STEP INTO THE WISDOM LANE OF WEALTH

*Unleash Your Intellectual,
Spiritual and Physical Potential*

Francis Adu-Donkor

STEP INTO THE WISDOM LANE OF WEALTH:
Unleash Your Intellectual, Spiritual and Physical Potential
www.wisdomlaneofwealth.com
Copyright © 2022 Francis Adu-Donkor

Paperback ISBN: 978-1-77277-515-0

All rights reserved. No portion of this book may be reproduced mechanically, electronically, or by any other means, including photocopying, without permission of the publisher or author except in the case of brief quotations embodied in critical articles and reviews. It is illegal to copy this book, post it to a website, or distribute it by any other means without permission from the publisher or author.

References to internet websites (URLs) were accurate at the time of writing. Authors and the publishers are not responsible for URLs that may have expired or changed since the manuscript was prepared.

Limits of Liability and Disclaimer of Warranty
The author and publisher shall not be liable for your misuse of the enclosed material. This book is strictly for informational and educational purposes only.

Warning – Disclaimer
The purpose of this book is to educate and entertain. The author and/or publisher do not guarantee that anyone following these techniques, suggestions, tips, ideas, or strategies will become successful. The author and/or publisher shall have neither liability nor responsibility to anyone with respect to any loss or damage caused, or alleged to be caused, directly or indirectly by the information contained in this book.

Publisher
10-10-10 Publishing
Markham, ON Canada

Printed in Canada and the United States of America

*I dedicate this book to every individual
who is cash-strapped and seeking a deeper understanding
of how wealth is created through divine means, and to the
wealthy who are saturated with wealth but have no clue
as to how to use it in a way that pleases God.*

*To those who lack confidence in their abilities to acquire
wealth, this book is dedicated to them. It invites them to pull
up their sleeves and dismantle all notions of inferiority about
their talents and capabilities. The principles highlighted in the
book pump life into minds that are defunct as far as hope and
inspiration for a brighter future are concerned.*

Table of Contents

Acknowledgements vii
Foreword xi

Chapter 1: Foundational Principles of Wealth 1
Chapter 2: Divine Mandates for Prosperity 19
Chapter 3: Principles on How Wealth Should Be Acquired ... 55
Chapter 4: The Mindset of Wealthy People 67
Chapter 5: Divine Signs You Are on the Path to the Wisdom
    Lane of Wealth 87
Chapter 6: Self-Destructive Thoughts about Wealth 107
Chapter 7: How We Lose Money Despite Hard Work 119
Chapter 8: Miseries of Wealth Without God 135
Chapter 9: Divine Attitudes Toward Wealth 149
Chapter 10: How the Godly Operate in Wealth 161
Chapter 11: Types of Wealth 175
Chapter 12: Things That Are Better Than Wealth 187
Chapter 13: The Synopsis: Is God against Wealth and
    Prosperity? 199

Divine Steps to Prosperity 207
Biblical Quotes on Wealth 209
About the Author 219

Acknowledgements

First and foremost, I would like to thank the Almighty God for His guidance on the topics I chose to elaborate on. This book is the brainchild of biblical teachings on wealth, and I cannot sidestep an acknowledgement to Him for His mercies and revelations.

This project has proved beyond reasonable doubt that the support and encouragement of the immediate family is indispensable. I am grateful to my spouse and children for their relentless support and encouragement. I could not have come this far without them. The confidence they instilled in me was overwhelming.

A sincere gratitude also goes to Bev Hills. Your words of inspiration meant a lot to me in moments of despair. Sometimes the task seemed tough to accomplish but you never pulled a pessimistic card, and you kept urging me to roll up my sleeves and accomplish the task.

The zeal to write a book was initially nourished by the recommendations of my colleagues at the Greater Toronto Airports Authority. Scripts of the "Weekly Observer" series sent waves of curiosity in readers as to who the author was. The lasting impressions of these scripts compelled most colleagues to admit their admiration for my style of writing and encourage me to write books. I am

For bonuses go to ...

therefore extending my sincere gratitude to all who set my passion to write on fire.

Walking back to the memory lane of my childhood days in school, I cannot lose sight of Dr. Lord Asamoah's mentorship. The writing skills he taught me at that tender age grew up with me, and this book is a fruit of his guidance. All the efforts he made years later to get me onto the highest academic pedestal, will never slip out of my memory.

It would be unkind on my part to keep a good friend, Dr. Robert Awuah Baffour, out of the limelight in these acknowledgements. He saw the potential in me to produce a classic book, and he kept nagging me to start writing when procrastination got the better part of me. Sometimes it takes well-wishers like Robert to initiate progressive attempts to achieve milestones in life.

Dr. Elizabeth A. Asante, of the University of Ghana, Legon, cannot be left out of these acknowledgements. Her belief in my ability to produce a book of this nature was a real source of inspiration. Nana Yaa, as I affectionately call her, was more than happy to be the first person to order a copy of the book after its publication.

A heartfelt acknowledgement also goes to Raymond Aaron and his team, especially book architect, Barbara Powers, and my editor, Lisa Browning. Barb has been a bastion of this project. I would tend to lose count of the number of times she would check on me to see how I was faring in every conceivable aspect of my life. There came a time when I lost all the scripts I had generated, due to a computer glitch. Barb's belief in my ability to reproduce them within the shortest possible time was a catalyst in the recovery process. I am grateful to Raymond for all the coaching sessions I was immersed in to become an authentic writer.

Mere words cannot express my gratitude to Christina Fife for the long hours she spent with me on the phone trying to sort out a better deal for my website.

Finally, my sincere gratitude to the publishing and cover page team that made this dream of holding a book in my hand materialize into shining reality. Mere words cannot describe my gratitude and indebtedness to the professional manner in which the book was published and publicized. May the Lord bless you all for your dedication to professional skills.

Foreword

Step Into the Wisdom Lane of Wealth by Francis Adu-Donkor is intended to show you that the Bible provides a guide on how to become wealthy. The scriptures not only include instructions on how to save your soul, but they also teach you vital lessons to avoid poverty on Earth. If you want to prosper in life and leave a legacy, God has laid down some ways that you can earn riches and honor from Him. The author unveils divine strategies that can transform your financial woes to a blissful life filled with wealth. Through diligence, knowledge, wisdom and self-discipline, you can dust off your financial woes and swim out of the sea of sameness you have been trapped in for years.

Francis shares with you his personal experiences on how he turned his rags around in exchange for riches, by following simple divine precepts. In this book:

- You will learn that wealth and prosperity stem from God, and that He is the source of everything.
- You will marvel at some divine principles that create wealth.
- You will see that management of resources is the fulcrum of wealth accumulation.
- You will get to know that there is a seed bag of potential in you that needs to be harvested.

For bonuses go to www.wisdomlaneofwealth.com

- You will familiarize yourself with how the godly operates in wealth

There is a great treasure buried within you that needs to be unleashed, and Francis demystifies the notion that you should stay poor on Earth and enjoy riches in heaven after you have passed on from this life.

Raymond Aaron
***New York Times* Bestselling Author**

Chapter 1

Foundational Principles of Wealth

THE SCOPE OF WEALTH

*"The earth is the Lord's and all it contains,
the world and those who dwell in it."*
Psalm 24:1

The Scripture quoted above is a striking illustration of the fact that wealth, which is part of the things our Earth contains, is owned by God. If it is owned by God, then it means that there is a spiritual element attached to it. Therefore, whoever is thirsty for the acquisition of wealth needs to quench this thirst by delving deep into the Bible, which is God's prescribed textbook of guidance in all spheres of life for the human race. This same verse quoted above also illustrates the fact that we were created by God. In other words, we are His products since we were manufactured by Him. As we all know, all manufacturers have user guides or manuals that guide consumers on how to handle their gadgets in such a way that they will function efficiently according to the purpose for which they were made. A critical look at the Bible indicates the same function as manuals, with all kinds of dos and don'ts just to ensure that we function appropriately and efficiently according to the purpose for which God created us.

For bonuses go to ...

A casual glance at the Bible may send us wrong signals about the acquisition of wealth. As a matter of fact, lots of denominations preach against wealth and portray it as something Christians should not indulge in. But a deeper look at wealth in the Bible indicates that prosperity is a blessing from God and that we were created to be wealthy enough to be able to accomplish God's work on Earth. Consequently, *Step Into the Wisdom Lane of Wealth* is an attempt to discredit the notion that Christians should remain poor so that they can go to Heaven and enjoy wealth. What the Bible rather teaches is that wealth gained through a godly manner is laudable. However, what it strongly cautions against is wealth obtained through dubious and evil schemes, and it gives blueprints to be followed in order to acquire wealth. Furthermore, the Scriptures highlight the dangers associated with the acquisition of wealth. It considers wealth as the most powerful thing in the world and, as a result, it can lead us astray from our faith. Lastly, there are prescribed obligations that wealth should fulfill. This book shines light on all these principles regarding ways of acquisition, preservation, usage and precautionary measures that need to be taken to ward off the curses associated with the wrong use of wealth.

The biblical perspective we gain is that there is nothing wrong with the acquisition of wealth. The problem emerges only when our wealth begins to own us in such a way that we become biblical fools by investing all our trusts, hopes and reliance in our acquired possessions. Money is a very lousy god; therefore, we need divine wisdom to guide us through the maze of acquiring it, keeping it and using it to the glory of God. This is all that the book is about: navigating the relationship between wisdom and wealth. One major characteristic of a wise man is the manner in which he handles money. As a matter of fact, wisdom is not revealed by the amount of money we possess, but by our frame of mind toward money, by the way we acquire it, and by the manner in which we use it. The book therefore explores the mindset of the wise toward wealth, and a probe into the ways in which money should be acquired and used.

WEALTH IS A LOUSY GOD AND NEEDS TO BE HANDLED WITH CARE

When we come to understand that God owns everything, then we will be inclined to believe that the Bible is the best financial guide for all and sundry, whether we are godly or ungodly. Earthly wealth, we are told, has no eternal value.

"When you set your eyes on it, it is gone. For wealth certainly makes itself wings, like an eagle that flies toward the heavens"
Proverbs 23:5

Anything we set our hearts on becomes an idol of worship, and that has a strong tendency to lead us into a life of spiritual anarchy. The moment we set foot on the path to prosperity, we tend to become spiritually paralyzed, thinking and believing that our wealth will take care of us. Our focus begins to shift to a materialistic view of existence that is short-lived compared to spiritual wealth, which is eternal. Divine wisdom is the fulcrum around which wealth revolves. The Bible says: ***"How much better is it to get wisdom than gold! And to get understanding is to be chosen rather than silver!"*** **(Proverbs 16:16)**

For bonuses go to ...

God's original plan was to extend His kingdom to the earth. When Jesus was asked to teach how to pray, He said, **"Our Father who art in heaven, hallowed be thy name; thy kingdom come; thy will be done on earth as it is in heaven..." (Matthew 6:9-10).** And we all know how a kingdom's concept of government works. The earth is a territory of the kingdom of God. This means that it is a domain over which the king exercises authority. The king owns everything in a kingdom and is obligated to care for and protect all of his citizens, whose welfare is a reflection of the king himself. The laws of a kingdom are the ways by which the citizens are guaranteed access to the benefits of the king and the kingdom, and they must be obeyed by all. These laws cannot be changed nor modified by the citizens. Obedience to the laws guarantees success to all citizens. In a word, territories are the exact replica of the kingdom. There is no poverty in heaven, so if we have a natural aversion to wealth, then we should never entertain the idea of going there.

The point I am striving to reach is that wealth is God's, and He has blueprints for us to follow in order to become prosperous. Since wealth is a miniature god, the Bible highlights the dangers associated with it and teaches us how to tame them in order to enjoy it in a way that is pleasant in the sight of the Lord. **Matthew 6:24 says: "No man can serve two masters: for either he will hate one, and love the other, or else he will hold to the one, and despise the other. You cannot serve God and mammon."** This verse reveals that money is capable of competing with God for allegiance and, as such, we need to be very careful in the way we acquire it, the way we spend it and our general attitude toward it. Obedience to the divine laws governing riches will guarantee our prosperity if applied to the letter. Any concepts or precepts regarding wealth acquisition and its usage should be sought from His manual, which is the Bible.

When we accept that wealth is God's instead of ours, we will be better equipped to manage it satisfactorily according to divine standards and principles. But there is one remarkable aspect everyone needs to know when it comes to managing our wealth biblically. Biblical management of wealth calls for wisdom! Brooding over financial woes sweeps us off the currents of helpless fears and anxiety. But turning to God for direction is what brings financial breakthroughs. **Proverbs 1:32** says: *"The prosperity of fools shall destroy them."* Throughout the scriptures, we notice that God wants us to experience blessings of prosperity. As a matter of fact, we cannot be effective at what God has called us to do unless we prosper and increase in the kingdom of God. So, the key to not being destroyed by wealth is to not be fools but to be filled with divine wisdom. Let us therefore ease into a wealth state of mind by reading this book for ideas on how to become wealthy through the divine lens of our Creator.

PHILOSOPHICAL QUESTIONS THAT DEFINE US

Every human being on Earth is battling with three philosophical questions in life. You can never become wealthy till you know the answers to them. They are so important that they control the entire world, and every human activity is motivated by these questions. The answers to them define who you are, what your purpose on Earth is and what your destiny will be. Without a purpose, life is meaningless. The billionaire as well as the poorest man living in slums is saddled with these philosophical questions. The first one is, where do we come from or what are our origins? Well, some people believe they came from a monkey and later developed into a man. There are lots of reasons out there; we know. The second question is, why are we here? And this is a very tough question because the ordinary human being has no clue as to why we are on Earth. The third one is, where are we going? In other words, what is our destiny?

Answers to these puzzling questions give us an identity, a purpose and a destiny. A look at the design in the universe indicates intelligence behind everything. If we look at how our mothers conceive and bring forth babies after nine months, we cannot deny the fact that someone designed birth. We couldn't have come to Earth through a blind chance. Genesis teaches that God created humanity, male and female, in His image and likeness. We are therefore divinely separated into male and female. So, there is a God who brought us into existence: **"Male and female, created He them" (Genesis 5:2).** When we look at a clock carefully, we can easily see intelligence behind how it works, just as how the human body functions; but most people never want to believe in God, because of folly. **Psalm 53:1** says: **"The fool has said in his heart that there is no God."** Believing in a creator gives us meaning in life. We are here on Earth because God has a purpose for us to fulfill. His aim is to make us wealthy so that we can accomplish His goals of helping the needy, worshipping Him and supporting His work of salvation. One thing that strikes me is that we are mortal beings made out of clay, and because of our sins, we are all bound to die. He says He made us out of the dust, and we shall return to dust till such time that He will create a new Heaven and a new Earth that is devoid of sin and death. **Psalm 144:4** also says: **"Man is like a**

breath; his days are like a passing shadow." Let us not lean on our worldly-acquired knowledge and reject divine knowledge. The one who manufactured us knows how mortal we are, and our fate as human beings is graphically depicted in the Bible.

Dear reader, I am not trying to shove a belief in God down your throat, but to be wealthy, you need to know the source of wealth and its owner. That will give you a purpose to live well and effectively. Despite all the signs that indicate the presence of a mighty being, I consider my faith in Him as an insurance policy for my life hereafter. Human beings are smart to insure their cars and homes against unforeseen circumstances, but they are not willing to insure their souls for the sake of eternal life. Some believe that death is the final stage of their lives, so they live anyhow; but the Bible says: ***"As it is appointed unto men once to die but after this the judgement"*** **(Hebrews 9:27).** We are cautioned to lead a responsible life because we will give an account of how we lived our lives one day, including the wealth that He blesses us with. All you have to do is just believe in His word and obey His commandments. Everybody is chasing money, but the scripture says: ***"Money is worthless when you face God's punishment"*** **(Proverbs 11:4).** Let us arm ourselves with the answers to these philosophical questions so that we can be wealthy. A belief in God shows where we come from; it gives us purpose to live, and it also defines our destiny in life on Earth.

For bonuses go to ...

GOD BUILT SUCCESS INTO ALL HIS CREATION

God designed everything He created, to be successful. For instance, you would never see a tortoise that cannot crawl or an eagle that cannot fly naturally. If you put a seed on the ground and water it, you do not need to fast and pray for it to germinate. This means that success in everything He created, including human beings, is very important to Him. He needs us to succeed because our failure constitutes a blemish on His image as a provider and a sustainer. That is why He gave us the Bible, to teach and guide us, just as manufacturers give user guides or manuals of their products to their customers. Only God knows how best we can function in order to be successful in life. Now the principle I am trying to share with you is that success is not guess work, and because it is predictable, you can literally plan it to play out how you want it to be. I am a living testimony of this principle for turning my rags to riches through obedience.

Let us look at how manufacturers ensure the success of their products. Just as God has built success into human beings when we follow His laws, so have all manufacturers built success into their products if the consumer follows the rules governing the use of their products. All manufacturers have a symbol on their products that represent the image of the company. For instance, Mercedes Benz has a silver circle with a three-pointed star in the middle, which represents the strength and reliability of Daimler engines all over the world. Before the vehicle comes out of the factory, they test it first to make sure that everything is working. They include a user guide or a manual and warn you to read it before operating the vehicle. Why? Because they know how it functions.

The manual is full of promises and guarantees, as well as instructions to follow so that the vehicle will perform as it should and last long. They guarantee you that the vehicle will perform as promised if you follow the orders given in the manual. For instance, they will instruct you to put only gasoline in the vehicle. Now, if you decide to put beer in the tank, will the vehicle drive as it should? It won't, for sure. Why? Because you violated the principle that needed to be obeyed for the vehicle to function as it should. This underscores the fact that only the maker knows how the product should be operated to ensure its success. Sometimes they do recalls when they detect a serious issue, and they fix the problem without charging a dime. Why? Because they want to protect their image, the success of their vehicles is of crucial importance to them. Whenever a product fails, the reputation of the manufacturer is at stake!

God created us. In other words, He is our manufacturer and that is why He has given us the Bible as a manual to show us how to lead our lives in order to be successful. Our failure is a blemish on His image. That is why He has given us commandments and principles to follow in order to be wealthy and prosperous. Disobeying these commandments will lead to our failure and ultimate death. Following them will guarantee our success and prosperity because obedience to laws makes life predictable. That is why success and prosperity are predictable. You can actually design your prosperity by following His commandments regarding wealth. God has to guarantee your success,

For bonuses go to ...

not to protect you but to protect His image as a creator and sustainer. In **Genesis 39:2**, we read that *"The Lord was with Joseph so that he prospered."* Do you want to be wealthy? Then draw closer to God, like Joseph, and He will give you the blueprint that will transform your rags into riches.

GOD DID NOT CREATE POOR PEOPLE AND RICH PEOPLE

"The poor man and the oppressor have this in common:
The Lord gives light to the eyes of both."
Proverbs 29:13

The vast majority of people have a twisted belief system about God. In the first place, they believe He is racist for creating some people black and some white. Moreover, they have a misconception that He created black people poor and white people wealthy. One thing they lose sight of is the fact that the diversity and unique nature of God's creation is incredible. Without a shadow of doubt, He created both the rich and the poor, as **Proverbs 22:2** says: *"Rich and poor have this in common: The Lord is the maker of them both."* Upon reading this, the question that lends itself for asking is, why then should a just God create some people rich and some poor? This question is very intriguing and is sarcastic at the same time, since He is known to have created all men equal no matter what their complexion is.

Walking back to the memory lane of my early days in Ghana where I was born and bred, scenes of abject poverty keep flashing through my mind. Most families were so steeped in poverty that putting meals on the table once a day was a tough task. Most children walked to school barefoot since most parents could not afford footwear for them. So initially, I was tempted to subscribe to the view that God does not like black people, till I came across **Proverbs 29:13,** which says: *"**The poor man and the oppressor have this in common: The Lord gives light to the eyes of both.**"* My wavering belief system was stabilized when I stumbled upon this verse. Having second thoughts, streams of clarifications began to drip into my mind. In other words, this verse seems to mean that all men were equally created by God, both blacks and whites. Some become rich and some become poor, depending on what they see and dream about. This revelation is very allegorical. One's vision in life determines one's future. What you see becomes your future, so a wealthy man is not better than a poor man. He simply sees differently. Two men may possess huge acres of land with the same measurements. One sees his as a flower production field, and the other sees his as a real estate development site filled with skyscrapers.

God created us equal with the same number of cells in our brains, and it is up to each individual to develop it in order to become wealthy. Having a concrete vision in life is one of the fundamental pivots around which wealth is built. Sometimes our lifestyles incur poverty for us. **Proverbs 23:21** says: *"**For the drunkard and the glutton will come to poverty, and drowsiness will clothe them in rags.**"* Here we see that a life of frivolity leads us to poverty. It is a strong indication of God's innocence about our misery. Moreover, we can say with all certainty that God gave us talents as well as the freedom of thought and action. Some achieve wealth with them, and others simply fold their arms and cruise in laziness. If we fail to explore our God-given gifts or talents, we will definitely end up being poor.

Deuteronomy 8:18 says: ***"And you shall remember the Lord your God, for it is He who gives you power to get wealth."*** A synonym for power used here is ability. And that means He has given all of us the ability and wisdom to be prosperous in life. As stated in a previous chapter, our prosperity is vital to our Creator because He created us in His own image, and our failure in life actually drags His name through the mud. So if you are one of those who think that God created rich people and poor people, I hope you will erase such a negative mindset instantly, and embrace the idea that He really wants everyone to be rich toward mankind and to God Himself by using our wealth to glorify Him.

Leviticus 26:3–4 says: ***"If you walk in My statutes and keep My commandments, and perform them, then I will give you rain in its season, the land shall yield their produce, and the trees of the field shall yield their fruit."*** This emphasizes the fact that success and prosperity are a result of obedience to God's laws. Therefore, they are predictable when we follow His laws on acquiring wealth.

WISDOM IS THE CORNERSTONE OF WEALTH ACCUMULATION

"For wisdom is better than rubies; and all the things that may be desired are not to be compared to it."
Proverbs 8:11

This biblical verse sums up the message in this book. It is loaded with the loftiest principle of wealth accumulation, and it also gives us a foretaste of what the wisdom lane of wealth entails. It brings in its trail some puzzling philosophical thoughts about wealth. Rubies are a deep-red form of the mineral corundum, which is valued as a precious stone. It is being used here to represent money. How can wisdom be better than rubies? This is very thought-provoking, and when I stumbled upon it, my whole mindset about the acquisition of wealth changed drastically. No wonder King Solomon opted for wisdom when God asked him to request anything he wanted from Him, at his enthronement as king of Israel. He pulled the wisdom card out of all the alternatives the Creator offered him and, in the long run, he became the wealthiest king that ever ruled Israel. This authenticates the validity of the scripture cited above.

Why is wisdom the building block of wealth and prosperity? In the first place, we have an adage that says that a fool and his money are soon parted. You may accumulate all the wealth under the sun, but if you lack the knowledge and wisdom to manage and multiply it, you will end up financially bankrupt. ***"The wise have wealth and luxury, but fools spend whatever they get"*** **(Proverbs 21:20).** There are countless numbers of famous sportsmen and women who earned millions of dollars during their prime of life, but they lost it all due to lack of wisdom. Some even landed in jail for petty theft. So, the wisdom to earn and keep money is a fundamental principle in stepping into the wisdom lane of wealth. *"Penny wise, pound foolish"* is another wise saying that underscores the relevance of wisdom in relation to wealth.

The Bible makes it clear that *"the fear of the Lord is the beginning of wisdom"* **(Proverbs 9:10).** Fearing God means giving reverence to Him and obeying His Laws. So if wisdom is the cornerstone of wealth and prosperity, then wealth is tied to obeying God's laws. **Psalm 119:99** says: *"Yes, I have more insight than my teachers, for I am always thinking of your laws."* Having more insight helps us to generate ideas to engage in wealth-producing undertakings. If you look at Steve Jobs (Apple Inc) and Bill Gates (Microsoft), what do you think is the basis of their billions of dollars? Is it not the wisdom to invent technological gadgets that have made life comfortable to the human race? **Proverbs 10:22** also says: *"The blessing of the Lord makes a person rich, and he adds no sorrow to it."* This is a classic illustration of the fact that wealth is strictly a matter of staying connected with godly principles. You don't have to live in debt or in fear of what the economy might do. There is financial breakthrough if only you will adhere to God's principles of achieving wealth, which will be addressed in the next chapter. I learnt them and applied them subsequently; no wonder my financial woes have vanished into thin air. Wisdom is knowledge in divine principles rightly applied, and that is the key to success and prosperity.

www.wisdomlaneofwealth.com

W.I.N.K.

To help you keep track of what you are learning from this book, I have provided a full page at the end of each chapter, with the acronym W.I.N.K. written across the top. It is an acronym I created, which stands for **What I Now Know.** On these pages, you can write your biggest insights, your favorite points from the chapter or even set goals for yourself, etc. It is simply a page at the end of every chapter, dedicated to helping you organize your thoughts and record them so that you do not forget.

For bonuses go to www.wisdomlaneofwealth.com

W.I.N.K.

Chapter 2

Divine Mandates for Prosperity

WORK

*"Then the LORD God put the man
in the Garden of Eden to work it and keep it."*
Genesis 2:15

Work is the prime injunction God gave mankind to become wealthy. As stated in the verse quoted above, the Lord put Adam in the Garden of Eden to work it and keep it. A research of the word "work" in Hebrew reveals an astounding aspect of it that should give us food for thought. In Hebrew, *work* means ***eragon.*** Interestingly, ***eragon*** means *to become yourself*. For instance, it is like a seed that becomes a tree. If *work* means *to become,* then the puzzling question we need to ask ourselves is, what does it mean to work in this biblical context? My understanding of it is that there is a huge potential of skills and talents that the Lord has embedded in each of us, which needs to be discovered to serve society. Therefore, work in this sense means there is a talent trapped in us that needs to be discovered, refined and dished out to the world as a solution to myriads of problems plaguing mankind.

For bonuses go to ...

I fact-checked this aspect of work as explained above and came to understand why the ordinary jobs we do never make us wealthy in comparison to billionaires like Bill Gates, Steve Jobs, Jeff Bezos, Elon Musk, Michael Jordan, Oprah Winfrey... and the list goes on and on. And the reason for their wealth is not farfetched. They simply discovered their skills, refined them, became themselves and served the society with their products. There is something in all of us that we need to become in order to step into the wisdom lane of wealth. We have come to embrace the idea that only hard work in our daily jobs can make us wealthy, but we all know that our salaries just put us in a survival mode to make ends meet. Our salaries help us to pay our bills and put food on the table, but we sometimes even struggle to meet these goals despite our hard work.

There is an interesting verse in the scriptures that confirms my understanding of this aspect of work. It says: ***"If the axe is dull and its edge unsharpened, more strength is needed, but skill will bring success"*** **(Ecclesiastes 10:10).** This verse goes a long way to support the claim that hard work and skill are like two parallel lines. It shows that nothing meaningful can be achieved with hard work in comparison to skillful abilities. If we doubt this, let us compare how much we earn after working hard for eight hours at our jobs, and what Messi, Ronaldo, Tiger Woods and Lebron James earn after a game. There is just one thing that differentiates them from most of us. They discovered their God-given talents, refined them by training hard, became what they are supposed to be and entertained the world with their skills. The source of their wealth is not mere luck! They developed their potential to the fullest, and their prosperity followed suit.

It is time each one of us paused for a moment to reflect on our hidden potentials in order to become what we were created for. Our jobs handcuff us and prevent us from engaging in our natural gifts. To acquire wealth, our normal jobs will barely help us to attain prosperity. It is only through the development of our skills that success in life can be attained abundantly. God created us not only to barely survive but to be a blessing to others. To fulfill this assignment, we need to blossom with prosperity. Our prosperity is vested in the discovery of the gifts and talents the Creator blessed us with from birth. God placed in us every vital requisite to fulfill our purpose on Earth, which is to enhance His kingdom work, a mission that requires wealth to accomplish.

Our job salaries are someone's estimate of our value. We cannot blossom with prosperity from our jobs, because someone else is controlling our value. Salaries and pay cheques from our normal jobs simply ensure that we are in survival mode to pay our bills and survive. They are not enough to spill out excess money for us to help the needy in the community. Only our natural work and businesses can help us accomplish more for the benefit of society and the immense work of the kingdom of God. Keeping our jobs is good; don't get me wrong. But having a business aside is our main call. We need to be managers of our own so that we can call our own shots!

For bonuses go to ...

BUSINESS IS THE PRINCIPAL BLUEPRINT THAT CREATES WEALTH

"And God blessed them, and God said unto them, 'Be fruitful and multiply, and replenish the earth and subdue it and have dominion over the fish of the sea, and over the fowl of the air and over every living thing that move upon the earth.'"
Genesis 1:28

The Bible can be described as the best textbook on prosperity. Unfortunately, most religious people are reeling in abject poverty due to lack of implementation of the biblical wealth-building principles they read every day. It is paradoxical to see unreligious people become so wealthy by practicing the biblical guidelines to their advantage, whilst most religious people are still sinking in the boat of poverty. Business is a power originally intended by God for the benefit of humanity. The first mandate God gave to Adam and Eve in the Garden of Eden is found in **Genesis 1:28:** *"And God blessed them, and God said unto them, 'Be fruitful and multiply, and replenish the earth and subdue it and have dominion over the fish of the sea, and over the fowl of the air and over every living thing that move upon the earth.'"* The meaning of "be fruitful" in this context is twofold. Apart from the mandate to procreate and grow the size of our families, this verse is also pregnant with business ideas. It is a wealth-acquisition system with a business mindset that is bound to make us successful in life.

Owning a business is the major key to prosperity. A look at all the most successful people in the world indicates that they all own productive companies. Companies create employment opportunities for the masses. If God is commanding us to be fruitful, it means we all possess seeds of gifts and talents within us that we need to harness. Steve Jobs developed his gift of a technological savvy and ended up creating the Apple Company, which now employs millions of workers. Bill Gates is a classic example. Microsoft is one of the leading companies in the world now. The advantage of owning a business is that we can never be fired by any boss, since we are our own bosses. So, God is giving us a mandate to be wealthy as well. He wants us to be wealthy so that we can live lives that are full of abundance and prosperity, and also be capable of funding His kingdom work.

Spreading the gospel throughout the world involves money. *To be fruitful,* in the Hebrew language, means *to produce* or *to work*. Any form of business demands hard work. Work was originally not a curse. It was God's idea, which means it is an excellent idea that makes us prosperous. In **Proverbs 14:23**, it says: ***"All hard work brings a profit."*** He says He will bless the works of our hands, which indicates that we can expect more than a normal return on our work. This twofold meaning of being fruitful seems to evade many people, especially those in underdeveloped countries, and this explains why most third world countries are so poor. They only understand the procreation aspect of it, to the neglect of the injunction to produce, and that is a devastating trap.

To be productive is to discover your God-given gifts and master them in such a way that you become a person of value in order to serve the world. In other words, it means developing a relentless work ethic and setting up businesses of our own, like Elon Musk (Tesla) and

Jeff Bezos (Amazon). To be productive is to produce, and whoever produces constantly never runs out of his products, which in turn ensures a steady stream of income for building wealth. As a matter of fact, all business concepts in the world are fostered by production, and they seem to have applied God's biblical blueprint. Only religious people feel miracles from God can make them prosper, by praying day and night for God to rain money on their roofs every passing moment! But listen to the answer Christ gave to some Pharisees and teachers who came to Him to ask for a miracle so that they could believe Him. He said: **"A wicked and adulterous generation asks for a sign" (Matthew 12:29).**

In other words, folding our arms and cozily spending lengthy hours in prayer, and fasting for prosperity, is not the Creator's blueprint for acquiring wealth. **Proverbs 10:4** says that *"idle hands make one poor, but diligent hands bring wealth."* Production sets the stage for financial success, and that is all the more reason the first commandment the Creator gave to our first parents was to work. The concept of work here is prior to the fall of man, when there was no sin on Earth. After the fall, the concept of work became tainted with pain and sweat as a punitive measure, but the idea is still the same. God has a strong aversion to laziness, and He loathes indolence to the core, and that is why the first mandate commands us to be productive.

Most underdeveloped countries are still financially shipwrecked because they are immersed in a culture of consumption and importation. Based on this injunction by God, poverty is actually due to lack of productivity rather than resources. The African continent is so blessed with material resources that it should have been the leading producer of several items in the world. But they prefer to import rather than export. It is high time this beloved continent woke up from its slumber and switched its mindset to export orientation, rather than the strapped import-oriented mindset. No wonder the United Nations Organization measures every nation's wealth by its gross national product. This means the nation that does not produce is called poor. The question that lends itself for asking is, what are we producing in order to join the wisdom lane of wealth? Poverty is the absence of self-production, because money does not make you rich but productivity does. **Proverbs 13:4** says: *"The soul of the sluggard craves and gets nothing, while the soul of the diligent is richly supplied."* Herein lies the secret of success and prosperity. Let us be fruitful in order to join the wisdom lane of wealth.

It is also high time Africans developed a business and managerial mindset. Most blacks feel they are incapable of creating their own businesses and managing them themselves. Most prefer to take up paid jobs as ordinary workers and be bossed around instead of striving for managerial roles.

MULTIPLY

"Dishonest money dwindles away, but whoever gathers money little by little makes it grow."
Proverbs 13:11

God's second blueprint for prosperity is to multiply. Whatever we have, whether it is money, talents, skills, knowledge or products we produce, needs to be multiplied. In the verse cited above, we find one way of increasing our personal wealth, and that is by saving our money little by little at the bank. The parable about the talents that Jesus gave, in **Matthew 25:14–30,** is a classic illustration of the importance of saving and investing our money for it to multiply. One of the servants who received a talent but decided to bury it incurred the disgust of his master. In the end, the only talent he had was taken away from him and was cast into utter darkness as a punishment for his inability to multiply his talent. Our Creator cares about our financial success because the Earth is a reflection of the heavenly kingdom, and poverty is nonexistent in the divine kingdom of God. This explains why He gives us blueprints to prosper in life.

The corporate world understands this mandate very well and that is why companies like Coca-Cola and MacDonald's are so prosperous. They have multiple locations all over the world, and all these companies seem to have hijacked God's principle. It is amazing to realize that all successful individuals and businesses in the world have implemented this key, and it has enabled them to reproduce their products millions of times. Based on this blueprint, businesses embark on global expansions by taking their operations into lucrative markets overseas. As a matter of fact, business expansion is a stage when a company seeks out more solutions to reach numerous customers and increase its brand awareness as well as its marginal profits. Another classic example of such companies is Wal-Mart. They have branches everywhere, and it has become so popular that each time a family needs to shop, Wal-Mart's name springs to mind. Companies of all shapes and sizes apply this biblical concept of prosperity

The Creator knows the best way we can prosper, and that is why He commands us to keep multiplying whatever we have and produce. The wealth of Warren Buffet stems from this blueprint of multiplicity. All he does is invest his money in the capital market. Investment is one of the most powerful tools of multiplying money. Albert Einstein was a brilliant scholar, who was amazed at what compound interest can do. Compounding takes a considerable amount of time, but the principle here is, "just do something." **Ecclesiastes 11:1** says: *"Cast your bread upon the waters, for after many days you will find it again."* This verse is a poetic way of saying that we should invest and diversify our resources. It is also a figurative way of saying "the casting of seeds on irrigated lands," which ultimately leads to harvesting in abundance. The act of casting is also used here figuratively to indicate being diligently active.

Investing is a powerful biblical blueprint that is linked with the mandate to multiply, which God gave to our first parents in the Garden of Eden. And in **Luke 19:13**, it says: *"So he called ten of his servants, and gave them ten minas, and told them, 'Engage in business till I come.'"* Investment is a powerful key to prosperity. And the best way to invest is in houses and lands. That is the reason it is called real estate. In fact, it is the most powerful way to invest. Unlike stock markets that fluctuate every now and then and may even lead to the loss of our entire capital if we do not diversify the portfolios we have invested in, real estate investments are stable, and the compounding of interest in this sphere of investment is incredible.

Right from the beginning of creation, God never gave the patriarchs, like Abraham, money. He gave them lands. Depositing money for pre-construction projects with assignment clauses are incredible ways of building wealth. With assignment clauses, you do not need to arrange for a mortgage if you are not ready to buy the newly constructed home. So, you can transfer the ownership to a potential buyer and reap substantial profits you could never have earned by saving your capital at the bank. Some of these pre-construction projects take years to complete. The initial cost before being completed may be $200,000.00, but by the time it is completed, the original price might have increased to about $400,000.00. So, with an assignment clause, you can easily sell it to someone else and just walk away with your down payment plus $200,000.00. That is the beauty of investing in pre-construction homes! This way, you will be following the blueprint given in **Ecclesiastes 11:1,** which says: ***"Cast your bread upon the waters, for after many days you will find it again."***

REPLENISH

To replenish is to fill up again, and the technical term that aptly describes this mandate is to distribute. It is incredible to know that God's ideas are all business ideas. He wants us to replenish whatever we produce in order to sustain a constant flow of income. Mass distribution creates the need to produce more. Businesses make every effort to bring their products and services to the market and make them available for consumers by creating a distribution system. For the sake of increasing sales and brand awareness, they expand their distribution channels. No matter how good our product is or how many times we reproduce, if we lack an effective distribution system, our companies will gradually grind to a halt. Nothing destroys a vibrant company faster than a dead inventory!

On the flip side, starting a distribution company might also be a golden opportunity for us to step into the wisdom lane of wealth. In other words, we might have no personal products to distribute, but we can start a distribution company on our own, just like what Costco and Amazon do. These companies produce nothing of their own, but they are the biggest distribution companies, with branches all over the globe. Their business concepts are all based on the divine blueprint of distribution as a means of generating wealth. Jeff Bezos is now a billionaire because he saw the effectiveness of this biblical principle of building wealth through a reliable distribution system and implemented it.

God is inviting you to look critically into this wealth creation module in Genesis. All successful individuals and companies in the world have followed the Creator's wealth creation program. It is high time religious people also applied this blueprint to become wealthy. No wonder Jesus once said, *"... for the children of this world are for their own generation wiser than the sons of the light"* **(Luke 16:8).** The world holds God's principles of prosperity in high esteem and applies them completely, but believers just learn them and remain inactive in its application. Being a Christian does not mean we should be poor, because God wants everybody to be wealthy so that we can fulfill His assignment on Earth. That is the reason He has provided these blueprints for us, to learn them and apply them just like Jeff Bezos. Wisdom is the application of divine principles in life.

For bonuses go to ...

SUBDUE AND DOMINATE

To subdue is to bring under control, and to dominate means to govern or to rule. But it also means to master, in the Hebrew language. In other words, we were born to master something. Anyone who masters something will be chased after. If we don't find our spot in mastery, whatever we do will be characterized by mediocrity. This implies we must seek to become valuable experts in our fields of specialty. People chase value, and that is what they spend their money on, and the only way to become valuable is to focus on a specialty. God is giving us a business mindset in this mandate. We were born to dominate an area of gifting that the Lord has blessed us with. All we need to do is to discover these gifts on our own and have dominion over them. In other words, we need to be unique in such a way that people from all walks of life will prefer to come to us for their needs rather than someone else.

There are a couple of traits that we need to adopt if we are going to dominate our sphere of gifting. The first is specialization. It is said that a jack of all trades is a master of none. This means that specializing in a particular field is better than being a general contractor. What I mean by this is that, for instance, instead of being a carpenter who does everything, just specialize in office furniture so that big companies will look for you and only you if they need to furnish their offices. Likewise, if you want to practice law, do not become a general legal practitioner. Rather, specialize in criminology for instance, so that criminals will know specifically who to go to when they need a specialist in this field of law. Secondly, always add value to the clients who come to you. For instance, if you are an optometrist, you may want to serve your clients with hot tea and some biscuits whilst they wait for their turn. People love good experiences. There are numerous traits you can adopt to single you out, but let me conclude by adding uniqueness to them. For instance, if you are a hairdresser, just step outside and study some new hairstyles that make you unique among your competitors.

DILIGENCE

"Now it shall come to pass, if you diligently obey the voice of the LORD your God, to observe carefully all His commandments which I command you today, that the Lord your God will set you high above all nations of the earth. And all these blessings shall come upon you and overtake you, because you obey the voice of the LORD your God."
Deuteronomy 28:1–2

A basic divine prescription for ailments in poverty is diligence. Diligence entails consistency and persistence in hard work. A diligent person does not throw caution to the wind when it comes to pursuing his aims and ambitions. He makes careful and consistent effort to ensure that his dreams materialize.

As stated in the scripture quoted above, the individual straightens his or her ears to listen to the divine voice of the Creator in a bid to obey His statutes and commandments to the letter. Laws and commandments guarantee success. They protect our principles, visions and potentials. No wonder the verse says that the outcome of diligently obeying the Lord is a projection of our status above all nations of the earth. This is a blueprint for prosperity that we all must familiarize ourselves with. It continues to say that we will be immersed in untold blessings of the Lord that will even overtake us since we are diligently obedient to His will. What an incredible promise from a Creator that loves us so much that He cannot afford to see His created beings fail in life.

In **Proverbs 10:3–4,** it says: ***"... the LORD does not allow the righteous to go hungry, but He thwarts the craving of the wicked. A slack hand causes poverty, but the hand of the diligent makes rich."*** This is a promise that never fails if we invest full trust in the Lord. He says He will feed us to the point of satiety if we are righteous enough to obey His commandments by pursuing godly things. Apart from never going hungry, He also promises us prosperity. We will roll in wealth if we are divinely diligent. The only thing dependable in life is God's promises. They never fail. All other things in the universe are subject to change. To cap it all, He puts emphasis on a mandate that we all need to apply in our lives. And that is eschewing laxity. He says a lazy hand will always drive us to the bottomless pit of poverty, but a diligent hand will always be enriched. The absence of diligence in our work ethics will cause us to be perpetually poor.

In **Proverbs 13:4,** we read that ***"The soul of a lazy man desires and has nothing, but the soul of the diligent shall be made rich."*** Here, once more, diligence is brought to the forefront as a blueprint for prosperity. Our cravings without working diligently will not attract any resources but will always leave us nothing in our hands to live on. To sum it up, diligence is a divine key for prosperity, and we need to chase it all the time. Indolence or laziness is a taboo in the sight of the Lord. That is why the scriptures are cautioning us repeatedly to desist from it. When we combine passion, vision and diligence together, we are laying a bedrock foundation for inevitable success and prosperity in our lives. The three together are so powerful that we become unstoppable on our way to the wisdom lane of wealth. I am a living testimony of the veracity in the potency of these divine prescriptions for prosperity. My life changed entirely, from living in the sea of sameness to a life of abundance, when I embraced the combination of all these precepts.

PAYING OF TITHES AND OFFERINGS

"Bring the whole tithe into the storehouse that there may be food in my house. Test me in this," says the Lord Almighty, "and see if I will not throw open the floodgates of heaven and pour out so much blessing there will not be room enough to store it."
Malachi 3:10

Tithing is God's management training academy for mankind, and the benefits of paying tithes and offerings cannot be over emphasized. In **Psalm 24:1,** the scripture says: *"The earth is the Lord's, and all it contains, the world and those who dwell in it."* This verse tells us that God owns everything, including our money and our whole being. So, why is He asking us to give a tenth of whatever we earn? Obviously, it is a test of faith in His ability to sustain us.. He is asking for a proof of our discipline, in putting aside a portion of whatever He gives for His work on Earth. If we can manage 10% properly, then He is elated to

For bonuses go to ...

trust us with the 90% that remains. But because we have been unfaithful with the 10%, we keep losing the 90% that is left. So, though we keep earning income bi-weekly, we keep losing the 90% and end up with 0% and sometimes even negative at the end.

Giving tithes or 10% of our income to the owner of the universe is among the most powerful success practices in the world. It began with the Old Testament patriarchs and has been used by lots of people to become millionaires, especially present-day Israelites. Abraham, Isaac, Jacob and Joseph were extremely wealthy because they relied on God as their financial sustainer. The scriptures say: ***"Thou shalt remember Jehovah, thy God, for it is He that giveth thee power to get wealth"*** **(Deuteronomy 8:18).** Jacob said this about tithing:

As we saw in **Haggai 2:8, *"'The silver is mine and the gold is mine,' declares the Lord of hosts."*** He has ownership of everything in the universe, but He commands us to give to Him so that we can always acknowledge the one who owns it. Whoever commands us to give has the authority to receive from us! A classic example is not farfetched. Just take a look at the income taxes the federal government levies on us. The government has the authority to deduct taxes from our income because it provides all the infrastructure and amenities we need in our daily lives. What about God who made us? Even the air we breathe alone, if He were to charge us, how could we afford our payments? He owns our lives and could invite us to our graves at any moment. Yet, He asks us to pay just one-tenth of whatever we receive.

According to the scripture cited above, He promises to bless us abundantly if we obey the commandment to pay tithes and offerings.

Offerings are liberal money we give to Him for His work on Earth, and so there is no stipulated amount given for its payment. What happens after paying our tithes and offerings is that He does not pour money on our roofs right away, but He rather gives us wisdom and ideas that will help us create businesses and undertake some financial projects that will yield income surplus for us. Why? Because He has checked and seen that you are obedient to His laws and that you are also faithful and trustworthy. **Isaiah 48:18** says: *"If only you had paid attention to my commandment! Then your well-being would have been like a river, and your righteousness like the waves of the sea."*

Some of the blessings He bestows upon us are in the form of good health and protection from disasters. You see, till such time that we grasp the concept of God's ownership of the universe, we will find it tough to observe His law concerning tithes and offerings. We tend to hold on to our wealth and other possessions as our own. But in a twinkle of an eye, He can wipe us out of this world, and what will become of all the stuff we think we owned? We came to the world empty handed when we were born, so nothing we acquire here is ours. The proof of this principle is the fact that we take nothing with us when we return to our graves.

Did you know there are curses associated with breaking this law on tithes and offerings? The scripture says, in **Malachi 3:8–9:** *"Will a mere mortal rob God? Yet you rob me. But you ask, 'How are we robbing you?' In tithes and offerings. You are under a curse—your whole nation—because you are robbing me."* The blueprint of tithes and offerings is a powerful gear that will help you switch easily into the wisdom lane of wealth. Do you wonder why the Israelites'

For bonuses go to ...

population is small, but the majority of the wealthiest people on Earth are all Israelites? If you ask them, they will reveal to you the powerful undercurrent that is causing the surge in their wealth. God's commandment on tithes and offerings is not only meant for physical Israelites; it is meant for us all, who are now spiritual Israelites.

The power inherent in this commandment is so incredible that refusal to obey it entails unimaginable financial disasters. As a matter of fact, our salvation is partially tied to the payment of tithes and offerings. Why? Because they are a measuring rod of your spirituality in honesty, accountability, trustworthiness and faithfulness toward God. It takes honesty to pay tithes because you can lie to anybody else but only God knows if you are truthful. And for you to manage a tithe, God has to trust you every moment. It also takes divine discipline to put aside 10% of your earnings for God's work.

So tithing helps us in a variety of ways. It hands us a management degree for our finances. It makes us diligent, disciplined and faithful in our responsibilities toward God. And it also makes us rich in the divine universe. **Matthew 6:19–21 says:** *"Do not store up for yourselves treasures on earth, where moths and vermin destroy, and where thieves break in and steal. But store up for yourselves treasures in heaven, where moths and vermin do not destroy, and where thieves do not break in and steal. For where your treasure is, there your heart will be also."* We can accomplish this through our tithes and offerings. The wealth we hoard on Earth cannot save us when death strikes! If we believe that it is God who gives us the ability to work, invest and multiply our money, then we need to take cognizance of the fact He owns everything we have. Consuming our riches for ourselves and putting our trust in our wealth will lead us nowhere. In **Matthew 19:24,** the scriptures say: *"It is easier for a camel to go through the eye of a needle, than for a rich man to enter into the kingdom of God."* This verse conveys a strong warning to the wealthy, simply because the possession of wealth makes us vulnerable to a lifestyle that runs parallel to the Creator's ethical principles.

Giving is a biblical wealth creation principle. When we pay our tithes and offerings, God gives us the ability to work hard and smartly, according to His word in **Luke 6:38:** *"Give and it will be given to you. A good measure, pressed down, shaken together and running over, will be poured into your lap. For with the measure you use, it will be measured back to you."* Giving to the Lord is a privilege to us in showing how grateful we are for His blessings. And as long as we pay our tithes and offerings, we cannot be greedy or needy. It demonstrates our faith in God as our source and sustenance of life. He blesses us abundantly. There is an adage that always pours showers of encouragement on me to give, and it says there has never been anyone who has become poor by giving. Psalm 95:2 says: *"Let us enter His presence with Thanksgiving."* Neglecting this command brings in its trail nothing but curses!

For bonuses go to ...

MANAGEMENT OF RESOURCES

*"Now no shrub had yet appeared on the earth,
and no plant had yet sprung up, for the Lord God had not sent rain
on the earth and there was no one to work the ground."*
Genesis 2:5

This verse encodes the reason God created mankind. It says that God put a screeching stop to everything He was doing because He had no one to manage His creation. It is therefore not surprising that the creation of man took place right after this verse. We saw earlier on in **Genesis 1:28** that mankind was to ***"have dominion over the fish of the sea and over the birds of the heavens and over every living thing that moves on the earth."*** God wanted this to occur through management. The mandate to manage indicates that we are mere stewards and that we do not own anything here on Earth.

This verse is also pregnant with lots of managerial concepts. Firstly, it indicates that God keeps a keen eye on His resources, and so He requires good managers to oversee them. The wealth we possess is His, and it behooves us to be trustworthy stewards. Good management is the key to sustaining the wealth we acquire. We are all witnesses of this fact in the way we handle money. The old adage says that a fool and his money are soon parted. This tells us that management is the key to retaining our hard-earned money. So, we cannot build wealth if we cannot manage our resources well. The earth is a colony of heaven, where optimal management is in the hands of God, and since He created us in His own image, He wants us also to be good managers. There are shocking examples of people who

www.wisdomlaneofwealth.com

won millions of dollars in the lottery but ended up in slums because they mismanaged their funds. Money is easy to get, but if it cannot stay and keeps running away from us, then it means there is something wrong with us. In other words, it means we cannot manage.

Management entails economizing the little we have. In other words, we need to get the maximum out of the minimum. Jesus illustrated this managerial skill with the parable of feeding 5000 people with five pieces of fish and two loaves of bread. We should always live within our means. Avoiding waste of resources is another managerial principle the scriptures teach us. In **John 6:12**, He gave a classic example of the importance of avoiding waste. After the crowd was fed, He asked the disciples to go round and collect the crumbs that had fallen to the ground. He said, *"Gather the pieces that are left over: Let nothing be wasted."* So the divine principle we learn from this is that we should not waste our resources.

"Penny wise, pound foolish" is a very popular adage, which indicates that earning lots of money is not the key to prosperity but rather managing it. To step into the wisdom lane of wealth, we need to gain control over our money through excellent management; otherwise, the lack of it will forever control us. The best way to manage our resources properly is to grasp the biblical view of how to manage money, and a deep understanding of how to use it the way God originally intended it to be used. Excellent money management is of prime importance to the Creator because He views it as a tool and resource to be properly managed for His work on Earth.

Another managerial skill the Bible teaches, is counting the cost before engaging in any financial venture. **Luke 14:28** says: ***"For which of you, desiring to build a tower, does not first sit down and count the cost, whether he has enough to complete it?"*** This verse is saturated with financial planning ideas. It teaches that we need to have a budget for everything we do so that we do not get stuck along the way and get mocked by onlookers. We need to save up substantially for any financial project we are undertaking. This is what is termed as planning.

The Creator's tactical ploy for guaranteeing our future prosperity is planning. Planning is a divine precept that serves as a gateway to financial prosperity. As a matter of fact, it is the building block of an organized life, and we need to capture the essence and priority of planning so that we can carve out the future we want. Through planning, our futures can be designed by ourselves and it helps us to take full control of the unknown.

The scriptures say that it is God who makes our plans succeed if we make and commit them to His care. **In Psalm 20:4**, David says: ***"May He give you the desire of your heart and make all your plans succeed."*** So here, we learn that planning is a divine injunction, and the Lord can establish our plans if we entrust them to Him. However, since He knows what is best for us, Proverbs 19:21 says: ***"Many are the plans in a person's heart, but it is the Lord's purpose that prevails."*** And His purpose for mankind is well-defined in the Bible. **Jeremiah 29:11** gives us a hint: ***"For I know the plans I have for you, declares the Lord, plans to prosper you and not to harm you, plans to give you hope and a future."*** These words that were spoken by God through Jeremiah indicate that the Creator Himself is a strategic planner, and it is His plans that give us hope. This emphasizes how critical planning is. Adversities are part of life, but with planning, we can shape the kind of future we crave for our lives.

Planning is a concrete path to wisdom. **Proverbs 6:6** says: ***"Go to the ant, you sluggard; consider her ways and be wise."*** This verse teaches us that planning prepares us to face the future squarely. Verse 8 of the chapter illuminates what the ant does: ***"... yet it stores its provisions in summer and gathers its food at harvest."*** Here, we see the ant using strategic thinking to plan its life to be able to face changes and adversities boldly. It does not want to be a victim of the seasons. By failing to plan and prepare, we are planning to fail in life. There is a big difference between dreamers and planners; this difference lies in the fact that planners translate their dreams into concrete reality, while dreamers stifle their hopes and aspirations by not planning.

Hope is not a plan. Good luck is what occurs when chance meets with planning. We need to plan ahead all the time. It had never rained when Noah was building the ark. Our aims and aspirations can only be attained through the channel of planning, and we must trust and believe the course by acting upon it. There is no other route to prosperity. A dream without planning is a mere wish. Planning is like a GPS; it shows our final destination as well as the best way to get there. It can be compared to the act of bringing our future prosperity into the present so that we can do something concrete about it now.

The adage goes that by failing to plan, we are planning to fail. Planning therefore makes our future predictable. We do not repair roofs when it is raining; rather roofs are repaired when there is sunshine. And that is exactly what planning is all about: preparedness toward adversity! We have to get a plan. And God wants us to commit our plans to Him so that they will succeed.

TRUSTING GOD AS OUR ONLY SOURCE OF WEALTH

> *"And my God shall supply all your needs*
> *according to His riches in glory by Christ Jesus."*
> **Philippians 4:19**

This key principle of wealth creation requires a strong faith in God as our provider. The Lord says, in **2 Thessalonians 3:10:** *"... The one who is unwilling to work, shall not eat."* This implies that God created work and commanded us to work to be able to eke out a living as our basic source of financial sustenance. Nevertheless, He never intended for us to invest our faith and hope of sustenance in work alone. Furthermore, He never intended for us to convert everything else, such us our credit cards, our families and social assistance from the government, into our source. God is our financial backbone. He is the wellspring of all our supplies. In **Matthew 6:26**, it says: *"Look at the birds of the air. They do not sow, nor do they reap, nor do they gather into barns, and your heavenly Father feeds them. Are you not much more valuable than they?"*

God supplies everything we need to thrive on. The scriptures never say that God makes us wealthy. **Deuteronomy 8:18** makes this clear. It says: *"But remember the Lord your God, for it is He who gives you the ability to produce wealth, and so confirms His covenant, which He swore to your ancestors…."* This illustrates the fact that God will always give us ideas, skills, gifts, concepts and abilities that will generate blessings of all forms and shapes to sustain us. **Proverbs 10:22** says: *"The blessings of the Lord, it maketh rich, and He addeth no sorrow with it."* The clue to permitting God to be our source of sustenance is to discover our natural gifts and talents. After discovering them, we need to tap them, specialize in them and accomplish them with a faithful heart.

We do not have to bear the weight of our provisions and supplies on our own shoulders, because our living has already been earned by the Lord. **Philippians 4:19** says: *"But my God shall supply all your need according to His riches in glory by Christ Jesus."* When we become convinced about this assurance from God, we can truly be a blessing to others and can therefore live a life of rest. All we need is a solid trust in His providence. The life of the Israelites exemplifies. They did not take the Promised Land when they were supposed to, because they feared the inhabitants instead of trusting God to deliver them. To them, the men of the land were giants and extra powerful, simply because they lost sight of the fact that all power belonged to God. Nevertheless, God was the one who miraculously saved them from the oppressive Egyptians and provided all their needs in the desert. When we reach a point in our lives when our sole trust is in God, all odds notwithstanding, and desist from looking up to others for providence, we become free to live life in abundance. That is when the Lord will prove His ability to sustain us. **Psalm 118:8–9** says: *"It is better to trust in the LORD than to put confidence in man. It is better to trust in the Lord than to put confidence in princes."*

POSSESSION OF LAND OR REAL ESTATE

"... fill the earth and subdue it; and have dominion....."
Genesis 1:28

The first commandment God gave to Adam and Eve was to fill the earth and have dominion over everything. All through the Bible, land possession is seen as the most valuable gift God gave to patriarchs like Abraham, Noah, Isaac, Jacob and Adam as well. In **Genesis 2:15**, the scriptures say: *"Then the Lord God took the man and put him into the Garden of Eden to cultivate it and keep it."* So, the first present God gave Adam, our forefather, was real estate. The Lord did the same with Abraham: *"The Lord said to Abram, after Lot had separated from him, 'Now lift up your eyes and look from the place where you are, northward and southward and eastward and westward, for all the land which you see, I will give it to you and to your descendants forever"* (Genesis 13:14–17).

Buying pieces of land is the sole investment the patriarchs are known to have indulged in. The moment Jacob set foot in the city of Shechem in Canaan, *"He bought the piece of land where he had pitched his tent, from the hand of the sons of Hamor, Shechem's father, for one hundred pieces of money"* (Genesis 33:19). God never gave them physical money but pieces of land. This teaches us that possession of land is the best source of wealth acquisition. And truly, real estate investment is the source of the wealth of most billionaires. In **Proverbs 31:16,** the wise king, Solomon, gives us the qualities of a virtuous woman. The most outstanding one in terms of prosperity is, *"She considers a field and buys it…."* That is real estate investment.

Appreciation or the rising of home values over time is how the vast majority of wealth is built in real estate. It is dubbed as the "home run" in many circles, when people make huge amounts of profit. While the stock markets and other forms of investments fluctuate, real estate values always go up in the long run, and it looks as if nothing can stop this trend since houses will always be in demand. Home ownership is a goal we should all strive for. Renting should just be a steppingstone on the journey to home ownership. A personal experience underscores this fact. I started life in Canada by renting an apartment in a slum area in Toronto. I was paying hundreds of dollars for a one-bedroom apartment. A time came when I stumbled upon biblical verses that recommended land ownership as a source for building wealth, so I started saving enormously toward home-ownership.

I have never regretted making that decision because my current situation, as an owner of four real estate homes in Ontario, is a product of that resolution I made to quit renting. Other ventures I made consisted of merely making a deposit on pre-construction homes with an assignment clause in the purchase agreement. This earned me hundreds of thousands of dollars even without going through the formal closing procedures. Buyers were ready to take ownership of the homes when they were completed, at higher prices than the original ones I had purchased them for; a fact that proves that possession of land is one of the fundamental divine principles of acquiring wealth. If we develop a home ownership mentality and start saving toward it with prayers, the Lord says, in **Hebrews 10:35–36:** *"So do not throw away your confidence; it will be richly rewarded…."* All we need is perseverance and hard work coupled with determination.

OBEYING GOD'S COMMANDMENTS

"And keep the charge of the Lord your God, walking in His ways and keeping His statutes, His commandments, His rules, and His testimonies, as it is written in the law of Moses, that you may prosper in all that you do and wherever you turn…."
1 Kings 2:3

God has created a wealth-generating system that cannot fail. The question that lends itself for asking is, are we operating in it? The only way we can operate effectively in it is by applying the knowledge, precepts and concepts He provides. And we can do this by obeying His divine laws and commandments as stated in the scripture quoted above. These verses are the instructions David gave to his son Solomon just before he died. The key element we glean from them is the guarantee of success and prosperity when we walk in God's ways. It is an assurance we can all rely on if we obey His statutes.

Principles and laws guarantee success, so we can actually predict success if we obey laws and principles. As we saw earlier on, work is one of the commandments of the Lord for prosperity. Anything that stops us from working violates the law. This is all the more reason that God loathes indolence. Each time we try to gain wealth without efforts, we are violating the law of work, and that is why the Creator does not like beggars. In **Psalm 37:25,** David the Psalmist makes an interesting observation regarding the righteous and how God blesses them: *"I have been young and now I am old, yet I have not seen the righteous forsaken or his descendants begging bread."* You see, God's word contains certain commandments and principles, which, when obeyed and followed, will keep us from being in a position of needing to beg from others.

It is noteworthy to realize that the righteous will always obey God's commandment to be hardworking. **Proverbs 20:4** says: *"The sluggard does not plow after the autumn, so he begs during the harvest and has nothing."* In this instance, the sluggard violates the principle of hard work. In **2 Thessalonians 3:10,** Paul gave this instruction to the brethren in Thessalonica: *"Make it your ambition to lead a quiet life and attend to your own business and work with your hands, just as we commanded you, so that you will behave properly toward outsiders and not be in any need."*

When we walk in the ways and statutes of the Lord, we gain wisdom and subsequently become wealthy like Solomon. **Leviticus 26:3–5** says: *"If you walk in my statutes and keep my commandments, and perform them, then I will give you rain in its season, the land shall yield its produce and the trees of the field shall yield their fruit. Your threshing shall last till the time of vintage, and the vintage shall last till the time of sowing. You shall eat your bread to the full,*

and dwell in your land safely." What an amazing assurance of prosperity when we obey the Creator's laws and statutes!

When the Lord is our shepherd, we will walk in His ways and shall not be in need of anything. That is exactly what Psalm 23:1 tells us. Work is the reason that we were created, so when we violate the rules regarding it, we become miserable in life and, therefore, resort to begging and borrowing to make ends meet. **Psalm 84:11–12** says: ***"For the Lord God is a sun and shield; the Lord will give grace and glory; no good thing will He withhold from them that walk uprightly."*** When we walk uprightly in the way of the Lord, which means when we obey His commandments, He will shine His light on our path, protect us and bring good things our way.

HONORING GOD WITH OUR WEALTH

"The blessings of the Lord bring wealth,
and He adds no trouble to it."
Proverbs 10:22

This theme recurs in almost every chapter because of its significance in rolling us into the lane of wealth. God is a giver, and since we were created in His own image, we have to be givers as well. As exact replicas of His image, He knows that we function optimally when we give of whatever we possess, and He is ever ready to reward us for that too. God is a giver of blessings, and we get His blessings bestowed upon us when we follow His ways, precepts and commandments, as we read earlier on.

There are several ways to honor the Lord. **Proverbs 3:9–10**, says: *"Honor thy Lord with your wealth, and with the first fruits of all thine increase. So shall thy barns be filled with plenty, and thy presses shall burst out with new wine."* We can honor Him through our worship by singing songs of praises. When we live uprightly by observing His commandments, we honor Him because others see Him through us. Our good works are also testimonials of whom we serve. But in this particular verse quoted above, it specifically demands us to honor Him with our **wealth**. It is when we honor the Lord with our substance, or wealth, that we enter into the wisdom lane of wealth. The verse mentions giving our *first fruits,* which is a reference to our tithes. Using our wealth in righteous ways, such us providing for our families' needs and engaging in works of charity, is inclusive. Ironically, all these forms of giving we immerse ourselves in, pave the way for us to amass more wealth.

The reason that we are obligated to honor the Lord with our wealth is not farfetched. **Deuteronomy 8:17** warns us not to say in our heart: *"My power and the might of my hand have gained me this wealth."* But **verse 18** says: *"... remember the Lord your God, for it is He who gives you power to get wealth."* We need to strike a chord of remembrance here, that all wealth comes from God. It is He who gives us the ability to generate wealth, whether little or much. Recognizing that our wealth is obtained through His power and not ours, creates a sense of humility and gratefulness in our hearts. Taking cognizance of this fact creates avenues for Him to shower blessings on our hard work through biblical wealth and prosperity. When we discredit God in this matter, we invite doom and curses upon ourselves. He cannot

For bonuses go to ...

divinely multiply our riches unless we recognize Him as the true source of all our wealth.

Proverbs 11:25 assures us that *"whoever brings blessing will be made rich, and he who waters will also be watered himself."* There are other forms of giving, such as being a blessing to others in our social circles. Such acts also unveil God's ability to ensure that we are blessed in exchange. The paying of tithes, as we saw in **Malachi 3:10–12,** is the most honorable way to give to the Lord, because when we give to the upkeep of the church, God opens up the windows of heaven, rebukes the devourer and stop the locusts from destroying our fruits. This will make others see us as blessed.

Honoring the Lord with our substance is like sowing and spreading seeds. **2 Corinthians 9:6–7** says: *"But this I say: He who sows sparingly will also reap sparingly, and he who sows grudgingly or of necessity; for God loves a cheerful giver."* Sowing little leads to a meagre harvest. In other words, if we are tight-fisted when giving to the Lord, our harvest will also be so sparse that we will consume all and have nothing left to invest and multiply our wealth. The flip side works contrarily. Spreading more seeds by giving more to the Lord allows us to gain more than enough to have surplus to invest. Finally, we need to give willingly and gladly, for the Lord loves only cheerful givers. Honoring the Lord with our wealth is a sure way of acquiring wealth and prosperity.

www.wisdomlaneofwealth.com

W.I.N.K.

Chapter 3

Principles on How Wealth Should be Acquired

WEALTH SHOULD BE ACQUIRED AT A PRICE

"Cursed is the ground because of you;
in toil you shall eat of it all the days of your life."
Genesis 3:17

The scriptures warn against the acquisition of wealth without a price to us. This could rightly be framed as the principle of labor and time. The pronouncement of a curse on the fall of man in the Garden of Eden is the foundation of this principle. Under no circumstances should money be sought without toil, hard work or our precious time. **Ephesians 4:28** says: *"Let the thief no longer steal, but rather let him labor, doing honest work with his own hands, so that he may have something to share with anyone in need."* When God tells us not to steal, He is actually telling us to make money honestly and not rip off other people's money. Furthermore, He is not simply telling us what not to do, but He is also instructing us what we should do with our money: to do whatever we can to help the needy in our society. He wants us to work faithfully and honestly so that we can share our resources with the poor.

For bonuses go to ...

We are all aware of the various ways we steal, cheat and manipulate to snatch other people's money and resources. The attitude and motives behind our actions are obvious. Behind all these vices lies the desire to have what belongs to others; to possess what we have not worked for and to get things for nothing. This is what ensnares people to casinos and racetracks as well as betting parlors and lottery kiosks. It is the same mindset that drives speculation in some financial ventures. The effects of such easy lifestyles are tragic. The zeal to get things without labor is the surest path to financial and moral ruin. **Proverbs 13:11** says: *"Wealth gained hastily will dwindle, but whoever gathers little by little will increase it."* Lots of people have won millions of dollars in the past through lotteries but have ended up living in slums within a short span of time. This indicates that biblical truths will always stand the tests of time.

Acquiring wealth at no cost to us connotes laziness. **Proverbs 20:13** says: *"Do not love sleep, lest you become poor; open your eyes, and you will be satisfied with food."* The opposite of diligence and hard work is indolence. Lazy folks have no zeal to work, but since they need to make money, they are obliged to resort to all kinds of schemes and get-rich-quick offers. The Bible teaches that all these other alternatives apart from honest work are bound to fizzle out. **Proverbs 12:11** says: *"He who tills his land will have plenty of bread, but he who pursues vain things lacks sense."*

WEALTH SHOULD BE ACQUIRED WITHOUT SACRIFICING OUR PRINCIPLES

"Ill-gotten treasures have no lasting value,
but righteousness delivers from death."
Proverbs 10:2

This scripture minces no words about the acquisition of wealth at the expense of divine principles. Because our whole moral fiber is composed of greed, envy and selfishness, we are prepared to go every mile to sacrifice our ethical values to gain wealth. The vast majority of people have embraced the old adage that says, **"The end justifies the means."** Such a principle in life does not sit well with our Creator. Many noble men have landed in jails because of bribery and corruption. Their ill-gotten wealth at the expense of their business ethics spelled their doom. **Proverbs 1:19** says: **"Such are the paths of all who go after ill-gotten gain; it takes away the life of those who get it."** In a variety of other verses, the Bible speaks strongly against gaining money dishonestly, so we have to be very careful with the way we earn it.

God promises that if we make efforts to earn our livelihood the right and divine way, He will provide for all our needs. **Proverbs 10:3** says: **"The Lord does not let the righteous go hungry, but he thwarts the craving of the wicked."** Our Lord and master, Jesus, taught his disciples to shun anxiety about life's battles. He made it clear that our heavenly Father feeds the birds of the air and that we human beings are of a greater value than the birds. With this assurance in mind, we should not involve ourselves in shady deals in our attempts to gain wealth.

WEALTH SHOULD BE ACQUIRED TRUTHFULLY

"Bread obtained by falsehood is sweet to a man,
but afterwards his mouth will be filled with gravel."
Proverbs 20:17

This scripture is filled with wisdom regarding choices and their consequences. Although bread is mentioned here, the emphasis of this verse is deceit. In other words, bread gained without labor or by unrighteous ways is an antithesis of **Genesis 3:19:** *"By the sweat of your brow, you will eat your bread…."* There are consequences attached to every dishonest means of acquiring wealth. In **Proverbs 21:6,** it says: *"A fortune made by a lying tongue is a fleeting vapor and a deadly snare."* This means that those who acquire wealth by lying are wasting their precious time since they are simply courting death. In reality, such people are not seeking wealth but rather death; and the riches they obtain will likewise vanish like their own breath of life.

WEALTH SHOULD NOT BE ACQUIRED AT THE COST OF JUSTICE

*"Better a little with righteousness
than much gain with injustice."*
Proverbs 16:8

At first sight, one may be tempted to see a glorification of poverty in this scripture. Conversely, it is simply saying that if we have a choice between having a little bit and God's ways, or having a lot and injustice and ungodliness, the choice for a little bit is far better. Righteousness depicts righteous acts and deeds, and it makes the assumption that doing the right thing might even cost us. Nevertheless, it is better to follow God's path and do the right thing rather than to acquire riches that might come to us if we push God's ways aside. Possession of wealth that is stained with injustice is a divine mistake. Each time we compromise our integrity for any gain, we prove that we lack moral principles in our lives and are therefore worthless in the kingdom of God.

Proverbs 13:11 says: *"Wealth gained dishonestly dwindles away, but whoever works diligently increases his prosperity."* In this verse, the wise man, Solomon, draws our attention to the difference between wealth obtained hastily and wealth gained slowly but honestly. This verse touches on both wealth that is acquired greedily or through doubtful means and that which is simply acquired instantly. If we seek wealth dishonestly by taking advantage of others or by indulging in schemes, we should expect our prosperity to vanish as fast as it came.

For bonuses go to ...

The other wealth being described here is money that has been gained through robbery of any form, swindling or cheating. A classic example of this is found in the Bible. Achan seized wealth in a dishonest way against the orders of God. What he acquired dwindled hastily and, when his sin was discovered, he was stoned to death. The scriptures are admonishing us that it is preferable to acquire wealth slowly but honestly. Another shining example of this principle is found in lotteries and gambling. Taking part in them in anticipation of winning mega prizes is a common vice that has gripped millions of people. Any attempt to gain wealth without effort nullifies God's prescribed means of earning income. Unfortunately, many of those who hit the jackpot, once in a blue moon, end up worse off financially after a couple of years than they were before they hit the jackpot. Since they did not labor to gain such fortunes, they lacked the wisdom to manage and protect it. Acquisition of wealth through unjustified means has dismal consequences.

WEALTH GAINED AT THE EXPENSE OF OTHERS IS AN ABOMINATION

"Do not rob the poor because they are poor,
nor crush the afflicted at the gate."
Proverbs 22:22

This verse warns against robbing the poor or crushing the afflicted at the gate. In those days in Israel, all financial transactions happened at the gate. The parallel of this is seen in our contemporary "Wall Street," where stocks are traded. The consequences of robbing the poor are clearly stated in the next verse: *"For the Lord will take up their case and will exact life for life."* Here, the Lord is saying that He Himself will plead their cause, so it emphasizes the seriousness with which God attaches to the acquisition of wealth at the expense of the marginalized.

In **James 5:4,** we read: *"Behold, the wages of the laborers who mowed your fields, which you kept back by fraud, are crying out against you, and the cries of the harvesters have reached the ears of the Lord of hosts."* This is another strong warning James gives to rich landowners who oppress the poor laborers who toil in their farms. He charges them of abusive use of them in terms of their wages. They would also be punished for hoarding wealth while they suffer in great need and misery. He describes their unpaid wages itself as crying out in the ears of the Lord against the oppressive landowners. These crimes include selfishness, abuse of their workers and indifference to their socio-economic plights. **Jeremiah 22:13** condemns this in stronger terms: *"Woe to him who builds his house by unrighteousness, and his upper rooms by injustice, who makes his neighbor serve him for nothing and does not give him his wages."*

For bonuses go to ...

RICHES SHOULD NOT BE ACQUIRED BY SACRIFICING RIGHTEOUSNESS

"Ill-gotten gains do not profit,
but righteousness delivers from death."
Proverbs 10:22

Ill-gotten gains are treasures of wickedness such as are obtained by any kind of unjust or twisted practices. In this verse, Solomon is giving a glimpse into a type of treasure that no matter how much it is worth, it is actually worthless. When we seek our treasure here on this planet, where moth and rust corrupt and where thieves break in and steal, we are just gathering up treasures of wickedness. The second part of the verse gives us an insight into a marvelous divine principle: **"But righteousness delivers from death."** This is a powerful and prophetic phrase for us. It is a treasure that can deliver us from the clutches of death. Inversely, any treasure that cannot save us from death is a counterfeit treasure, and it is not worthy of pursuit.

So, there is only one treasure we should aspire to gather, and the Bible tells us a lot about this kind of treasure. Jesus asked an interesting question in **Matthew 16:26: *"What will it profit a man if he gains the whole world and forfeits his soul? Or what will a man give in exchange for his soul?"*** The question that lends itself for asking is, what amount of money or earthly treasure can pay the price for our souls? The answer is not farfetched. There is no amount of money on this planet that is worthy of trading your integrity and godliness. All treasures acquired through unrighteousness amount to nothing before the Creator.

Righteousness is just one of the biblical priorities we should never violate to acquire wealth. Johann Wolfgang, a renowned German writer, said something interesting that is divinely noteworthy. He said, ***"Things which matter most must never be at the mercy of things which matter least."*** Our top divine priority of seeking the kingdom of God first, should never be compromised by indulging in unrighteous means of wealth acquisition. Neither should our character be adulterated by the love of money.

For bonuses go to www.wisdomlaneofwealth.com

W.I.N.K.

Chapter 4

The Mindset of Wealthy People

THE WEALTHY ARE VISIONARIES

*"Where there is no vision, the people perish:
but he that keepeth the law, happy is he."*
Proverbs 29:18

Stepping into the wisdom lane of wealth involves a thought process that begins with having the qualities of a visionary. Vision falls into two categories: namely, sight and vision. Sight is the power of seeing things as they are with our naked eyes, but vision is the power of seeing things as they could be. If you ask me what the most powerful force on planet Earth is, I will not hesitate a minute to tell you that vision is the answer. It holds the key to our prosperity, and the reason is not farfetched. Visionaries have the ability to see the invisible as a reality. Vision gives us the authority to engage in things others consider as impossible. It is having a clear-cut picture of the lifestyle you prefer to lead in the future, that is worth pursuing. It is a virtual showcase of our state in the future, so it gives us a glimpse into our purpose in life.

It is important to have a vision of what we really want to be in the future, because it is the gravitational force that controls our habits in

For bonuses go to ...

life, with the sole aim of staying focused on what we want to achieve for ourselves. In the verse quoted above, Solomon is saying that not having a vision means casting our self-control to the wind. In other words, discipline will be nonexistent in our lives, and without discipline, we will tend to lead lives that will not benefit us. Vision is the seedbed of our self-discipline. We tend to live simple but restrictive lives when we have a vision, because it holds us captive and steers our actions toward the fulfillment of our goals.

One characteristic of having a vision is that it attracts envy and jealousy, so we need to brace ourselves for antagonism whenever we reveal our vision. A classic example is what Joseph experienced in the hands of his own brothers. **Genesis 37:5** says: ***"Joseph had a dream, and when he told it to his brothers, they hated him."*** After revealing that, they were binding sheaves of grain in the field, when suddenly his sheaf rose and stood upright, while their sheaves gathered around his and bowed down to his. Let us look at his brothers' responses: ***"Do you intend to reign over us?"*** No wonder they tried to kill him at first but on second thought decided to sell him into slavery.

Visions are so powerful that we need to keep them secret to ward off hatred. Secondly, visions go through difficult examinations that are not meant to kill us but to test how committed we are to achieving them. A shining example is the afflictions Jesus went through on Earth. His main aim was to save mankind no matter what the cost. In **Luke 24:7,** it says: ***"The Son of Man is going to be delivered into the hands of sinful men, and he shall be crucified...."*** Though he had the divine power to overturn his fate, he kept his vision of our salvation intact. That is how real visionaries behave! They never take their eyes off their goals, no matter how scary the storms might be. Visions of becoming a millionaire might lead us to even declare bankruptcy, but we still have to get up from our financial pits and make it to the wisdom lane of wealth. We must be prepared to lose all prior to gaining all. That is the mentality of visionaries; nothing breaks their resolve to attain their goals.

I stated earlier on that sight is the power of seeing things as they are with our naked eyes, but vision is the power of seeing things as they could be. Let me illustrate this point with the sale of Alaska, by the Soviet Union to the United States, for $7.2 million in October 1867. Whilst the Americans visualized the potential in this vast strip of land, the Russians considered it as an economic liability. Shortly after the purchase of Alaska, rich gold deposits were discovered and the place was swarmed with gold hunters, from America in general. The Russians were shocked beyond description to know this discovery, but there was no use crying over spilt milk. This illustrates how powerful vision is. When visionaries see a forest, they do not see just the trees but a booming business of furniture. It boils down to saying that vision is the art of seeing what is invisible to others.

THE WEALTHY ARE DECISIVE

Decision making is the cradle of success and prosperity. This trait is found in all wealthy people. No progress can be made in life without making decisions. It is very interesting to know that our destinies are carved out in our moments of decisions making. One peculiar thing I have found is that the moment we know what our values are, making

For bonuses go to ...

decisions become easy. Our values dictate every decision we make. Sadly enough, whilst the poor make decisions based on their present condition, the wealthy and successful people make decisions based on their destiny or where they want to be in future.

As a matter of fact, it is our vision that helps us to make decisions in life. The greatest privilege God gave mankind is the ability to make choices, which is the ability to make decisions concerning how we lead our lives. Making good and divine choices that please God is the best alternative when exercising this power of choice entrusted to us. We must, however, bear in mind that the quality of our decisions is determined by the quality of information we have. Expressed in other words, our decisions could be as good as the information we have. The more knowledge we possess, the better the information we obtain to make quality decisions.

Decisiveness plays a key role in the acquisition of wealth. The word procrastination does not exist in the vocabulary of the wealthy. They make decisions quickly and confidently, but they also vary their decisions and adjust them promptly when they need to. Those who fail to acquire wealth are people who are caught up in the web of indecision. They are fickle-minded and can be compared to rolling stones that gather no moss! They talk too much and do very little. Aside from this, they keep procrastinating the necessary steps they need to take to translate their decisions into shining reality. In fact, the whole universe conspires to make room for people who are pragmatic, because their words and actions indicate that they know where they are going. Their actions weigh more on the balancing scales than their words. The wealthy really know how to make decisions.

The power of decisiveness will always compel us to chase our dreams and purposes. Sometimes the opinions of others play a vital role in plunging us into the hole of indecision. They tend to cast doubts on the success of our plans, which ultimately leads us to backtrack. Stepping into the wisdom lane of wealth requires firmness and tenacity in whatever we decide to achieve in our lives. As a matter of fact, we are all the end products of decisions we made in our lives. Success is a result of decisions. Whatever we are, we decided to become, so we should not blame others for our predicament. Failure in life is a result of decisions. Whatever we decide, determines our destiny.

THE WEALTHY ARE SELF-DISCIPLINED

"For the moment, all discipline seems painful rather than pleasant, but later it yields the peaceful fruit of righteousness to those who have been trained by it."
Hebrews 12:11

Those who are prosperous have a high sense of discipline, which is dictated by the vision they have vowed to accomplish. Discipline is therefore a set of self-imposed qualities and limitations we put on ourselves that are inspired by our aims and aspirations. It is when we become detectives of ourselves because we have a specific vision we want to achieve in our lives. Anybody who is devoid of self-discipline is at the mercy of uncountable destructive disciplines that the universe has in store for us. Discipline is the loftiest call of moral and financial order. The fact that discipline safeguards our vision makes it possible for us to form a character in us. Our visions are bound to fail if they lack a strict character we can adhere to in order to ensure we are pursuing the right course to materialize our dreams. It is all because our character stems from our vision when discipline is actively involved. Accomplishing our dreams takes a lot of discipline.

Self-discipline is a mindset that is motivated by a specific destiny. For instance, if we plan to become a medical doctor, we immerse ourselves in the study of the physical sciences, like biology, chemistry and physics. We spend our time qualitatively in the science laboratories by engaging ourselves in all kinds of experiments to ensure we are well positioned to practice medicine as required by our profession. If we want to become financially independent, we seek only avenues that open doors for us to acquire wealth. We make budgets that fit our resources and curtail all unnecessary expenses that tend to lead us into debt. It amounts to having control over ourselves. Self-discipline has lots of characteristics, among which is the ability to forego immediate pleasure and gratification in anticipation of a better future.

Being self-disciplined makes us opt for the right decisions and refine our thoughts, behavior and actions to achieve success and prosperity. Life has a propensity to throw challenges on our paths to financial freedom. To overcome these hurdles, we need to cultivate the habit of persistence and perseverance, which can only be obtained through self-discipline. If we are steeped in unproductive habits, self-discipline helps us gain mastery over them. The importance of self-discipline lies in the fact that it helps us organize, schedule and do things as planned. It creates consistency in what we do, and this acts as a catalyst in the achievement of our goals. It also molds us to become an improved version of ourselves. To achieve self-discipline, we need to revisit our visions and set concrete goals. Goal setting allows us to grasp a clearer picture of our needs for prosperity, and setting deadlines also acts as a driving force to focus on the means we avail ourselves of in order to attain our goals. In short, we cannot really achieve prosperity without the application of self-discipline in our lives. Through it, we end up nurturing our path to prosperity with self-confidence and inner strength. Anyone who lacks it, falls an easy prey to failure and financial disaster.

THE WEALTHY ARE OBSSESSED WITH IDEAS

"Remember the Lord your God,
for it is He who gives you the ability to produce wealth."
Deuteronomy 8:18

One major trait of wealthy people is the obsession of ideas. We are as rich as our ideas, and the antithesis goes for poverty: We are as poor as our ideas. When we obey the commandments of the Creator regarding tithes and offerings, He gives us the power and ideas to acquire wealth. Ideas are spark plugs for prosperity. Ideas are the life source of innovation. For a business to flourish, ideas play an essential role in creativity and development. The world is plagued with

For bonuses go to ...

uncountable problems and, to be wealthy, we need to be specialists in solving problems, which entails having ideas to solve specific problems. It is interesting to note that all the billionaires of our times gained their wealth through the solution of contemporary problems.

Ideas are the most powerful things on Earth. All great inventors and scientists utilized their ideas to change the way civilizations operate in our world. Steve Jobs' invention of the iPhone and iPad made the usage and portability of massive office desk computers possible for the human race. No wonder he became a billionaire despite being a college dropout. This indicates that we do not need to possess a master's degree or a PhD to become wealthy. God has given us a massive brain that is itching to be filled with ideas. It is like the hard drives on our computers: They remain empty till we upload stuff on them. Therefore, we are obliged to seek knowledge, understanding and wisdom, such as the business concept God gave us in **Genesis 1:28:** *"And God blessed them and said to them: 'Be fruitful and multiply, and replenish the earth, and subdue it, and have dominion over the fish of the sea.'"*

To be able to produce stuff and multiply it requires ideas. That is all that wealthy people do. They have ideas to develop computer software (Bill Gates); they have ideas to develop a distribution system that gets stuff delivered in the twinkling of an eye (Jeff Bezos); they have ideas to invent electronic payment systems and to launch vehicles and spacecrafts (Elon Musk); they have ideas to multiply money (Warren Buffet)—and the list goes on and on. The remarkable thing about these billionaires is that they use their God-given skills and talents to produce something that solves basic problems facing mankind.

The wealthy acquire wisdom, and the wisdom they acquire yields ideas, and the ideas they have, give birth to wealth. The advice we need to take here is that we should not seek money. What we need to seek is ideas! Most of the time, we become broke and penniless, all because we lack ideas to make money. All we need to do is put on our thinking caps! In times of financial and economic crisis, the wealthy never panic; they simply think of solutions to emerging problems. Thinking of solutions to existing problems is the gateway to prosperity. The vast majority of us are really trapped in a culture that commands us to seek paid jobs and chase money. A wealthy mindset discards this dream killing culture. Their passion is wealth creation, and that can only happen if we develop ideas to produce.

God is ever ready to bestow divine schemes, concepts, ideas and projects on us, and what we need to do is just ask Him. God does not give us money and wealth. He gives us the ability to produce and invent stuff. Let us pray to Him to open our eyes to see a wedding banquet in five loaves of bread and two fishes; help us to see renting apartments in our basements; help us to see a grocery store in using our huge backyards to plant fruits and vegetables; and help us to see pieces of furniture in the trees around us. In short, may our minds be filled with divine ideas!

For bonuses go to ...

PERSEVERANCE AND RESILIENCE

*"And let us not grow weary of doing good,
for in due season we will reap, if we do not give up."*
Galatians 6:9

A noteworthy mindset of the wealthy is their perseverance and resilience. Perseverance is the persistence in doing something despite difficulty in achieving success, and resilience is the capacity to recover quickly from difficulties. Wealthy people go through lots of setbacks, but they never give up. They possess a tunnel vision in the sense that their focus is their central point of vision, and they are resolved to let nothing lead them astray from achieving their goals.

Let us drill deeper for examples of such millionaires. Prior to establishing Ford Motor Company, Henry Ford declared bankruptcy and was left with no money several times from abortive ventures. We all know the famous Albert Einstein as a genius man. In his youth, he was not viewed as scholarly talented, so his parents and teachers entertained the thought that he was mentally challenged since he did not begin to speak until he was four years old, nor could he read till he turned 7. He was consequently sacked from school and denied entry to Zurich Polytechnic School, but he became one of the best scholars of his time.

Another prime example is Oprah Winfrey. One of the first jobs she landed as a television anchor ended abruptly after the producer affirmed that she was "unfit for television." Now, looking at how far she has come, that producer might be biting her finger in regret. The last but not the least is Bill Gates. He started Traf-O-Data, a business that created reports for roadway engineers, from raw traffic data. The business did achieve some success but, allegedly, the machine built to process the data failed completely when he tried to present it to a Seattle County traffic employee. This did not put a screeching stop to Bill's dreams, and the lessons he learnt from this experience helped him to create Microsoft.

To be resilient is to have the ability "to bounce back," so it is all about the development of strength and adaptability to withstand failures, challenges and setbacks. Resilience allows us to meander through challenges and hurdles in life and still go on to achieve wealth and prosperity. It is therefore advisable for all of us to possess this trait because it can help us move on from life's mishaps. Perseverance equips us to face changes and diversities in life squarely. It helps us to transform our winters into summers. It also helps to develop positive attitudes toward all kinds of financial weather.

SELF-DEVELOPMENT

"To put off your old self, which belongs to your former manner of life and is corrupt through deceitful desires, and to be renewed in the spirit of your minds and to put on the new self, created after the likeness of God in true righteousness and holiness."
Ephesians 4:22–24

One of the greatest traits of a wealthy mindset is constant self-development. Wealth is something we attract and not something we pursue. Staying wealthy is searching for a good spot to stay. So, instead of chasing money, the rich work on their personal development. In other words, they seek to make themselves more valuable. This explains why two people may be working in the same company but one may earn two or three times as much as the other. The key here is how valuable you are to the company you work in. Bringing value to the marketplace is how salaries are measured. Economically, we do not get paid substantially for the time spent, but rather we get paid for how much we are worth to a company. This explains why CEOs earn millions of dollars per year compared to the ordinary worker in a company.

The rich always develop an above-average intensity to gain more wealth. They make themselves like precious jewelry—so valuable that they get paid to share their gifts, talents and ideas. They are constantly moving forward, and they perceive their growth and development as never-ending. They are so committed to their personal growth that people who attempt to derail their progress feel scared and run helter-skelter before them. The wealthy do not follow the crowd; they engage themselves in what they love and follow their own way. And because they chase their dreams and visions, success and prosperity follow them everywhere. They view their personal development as a major time saver, and they are convinced that the better they become, the less time it will take them to attain their aims and aspirations.

The wealthy are always on a learning curve, and curiosity is their stock in trade; they are always asking questions and reading quality books. They also ensure that everything they learn is put into action, because wisdom is the application of knowledge and principles learnt.

Just knowing stuff is insufficient for them; they apply it. Their philosophy is that the best investment they can make is in themselves.

THE WEALTHY ARE GOAL SETTERS

"The plans of the diligent lead to a profit
as surely as haste leads to poverty."
Proverbs 21:5

As the verse quoted above indicates, planning your life ahead of time yields profits. One basic trait of the wealthy is goal setting. They consider it as the first step in transforming the invisible into the visible. They view goals as the GPS that directs their lives to prosperity. If we aspire to be wealthy, we need to set goals that will direct our thoughts, free up our energy and stimulate our hopes and ambitions.

Goal setting encourages us to set deadlines for whatever we wish to achieve in life. Surprisingly, the minute we set a deadline on our dreams, they become a goal to be achieved at all costs. Goal setting is like beginning with the end in mind. When we work it out, plan it out and dream it, we make great things occur. This explains why the wealthy are goal setters! It is one of their secrets to prosperity. They are strong believers that courage, coupled with goal setting and focus, will always land them in the wisdom lane of wealth.

If we do not set goals, then we are not aiming for anything; and if we are not aiming for something, then we will hit nothing as an achievement. Setting goals makes us plan effectively because a goal

For bonuses go to ...

without a plan is a mere wish. It is incredible what we can achieve if we set goals. They inspire us when we believe in them. And when we act upon them, the whole universe conspires to make our dreams come true. Our brains open a task list when we set goals to achieve.

To achieve our goals, we need to write them down and read them every blessed day. Furthermore, we need to set them very high and never hesitate to pursue them till we achieve them. Setting goals beyond our reach enables us to have something to strive for. The victory of wealth and prosperity is almost half won when we cultivate the habit of setting and attaining goals cast in deadlines.

Some of the characteristics of goal setting are clarity of aim, possibility of its achievement and its relevance in our personal lives. The questions we should ask ourselves regarding these characteristics are: Are our goals well-defined? Are they measurable or can they be valued in exact terms? Are they attainable? And lastly, do they have a deadline? If we want to be wealthy and prosperous, we need to have a belief system that dictates that the future will be far better than it is now, and that we have the wisdom and power to make it so. Without goals to achieve in life, there is no living. We will just be existing, but that is not the reason we are here on planet Earth. Albert Einstein once said something that really resonates with this particular trait of the wealthy. He said, ***"If you want to live a happy life, tie it to a goal, not to people or things."***

Finally, our plans and goals may not be in alignment with that of God's for us. Therefore, we should seek to understand what the Lord is calling us to do, and how to attain our goals. **Proverbs 19:21** says:

"Many are the plans in a person's heart, but it is the Lord's purpose that prevails." We need to take our goals to the Lord in prayer in order to discern His will.

THE WEALTHY BELIEVE IN THEIR POTENTIAL

"I can do all things through him who strengthens me."
Philippians 4:13

The wealthy believe that they are bound to face setbacks in their lives if they want to achieve prosperity. Therefore, they prop themselves up to overcome any hurdles that crop up on their way. They have faith in themselves, and they also believe in their inner strength, which is their potential to achieve anything they want in life. They believe that they have the power to achieve everything their hearts desire. They enrich their minds with this biblical quote from **Genesis 1:27:** ***"So God created man in His own image, in the image of God created He; male and female, He created them."*** This verse offers food for thought! If we were created in God's image, then it means we possess an incredible potential to achieve anything we want on Earth. No wonder He commands us in the next verse to ***"be fruitful and multiply, and fill the earth, and subdue it, and have dominion over the fish of the sea, and over the birds of the heavens, and over every living thing that moves on the earth."*** We need to believe in our ability to achieve everything we set in our hearts to do. God has blessed us with abilities to accomplish everything if, and only if, we have confidence in ourselves.

For bonuses go to ...

Sometimes we let memories of our past limit the potential of what we can become in the future. In **Philippians 3:13,** Paul says something interesting that should inspire us: ***"Brethren, I do not count myself to have apprehended; but one thing I do, forgetting those things which are behind and reaching forward to those things which are ahead, I press toward the goal for the prize of the upward call of God in Christ Jesus."*** We should not allow our past to put us in a cage. On our path to the wisdom lane of wealth, we should not envisage any limits to what we can achieve. Believing in ourselves is the optimum way to find our real potential. We need to stretch ourselves beyond our limits. We were born to be prosperous; but to be wealthy, we must plan to succeed, prepare to succeed and expect victory to come our way at all costs. Success is a virtue we demand from ourselves and not from someone else. We need to accept ourselves, no matter what, and keep advancing. If we want to fly, we need to sacrifice whatever weighs us down. We can never become who we want to be till such time that we accept who we are and be happy just as we are.

The discovery of our talents sets the pace of our wealth in motion. Till we release them into the flow of wealth, our talents and potentials sit idle in us. However, we can never maximize our potential till such time that we discover our purpose.

W.I.N.K.

Chapter 5

Divine Signs You Are On the Path to the Wisdom Lane of Wealth

5

THE FEAR OF THE LORD IS IN YOU

"Praise the LORD! Blessed is the man who fears the LORD, who delights greatly in His commandments. His descendants will be mighty on earth; the generation of the upright will be blessed. Wealth and riches will be in his house, and his righteousness endures forever."
Psalm 112:1–3

One of the most misunderstood phrases in the Bible is the fear of the Lord, because the minute fear is mentioned, most people think of the type of terror that scares us away and sets our hearts pounding. But that is not all what the fear of the Lord is about. To fear God is to desire to live in harmony with his divine principles, and to surrender our will to His will, and the Bible states categorically that the fear of the Lord is the beginning of wisdom. Anyone who has the fear of the Lord in his heart obeys His commandments and precepts. The divine fear that grips us makes us run toward him and put all our trust in Him for our sustenance. This fear melts our pride and produces confidence in us to confront any crisis in our lives. As revealed in previous chapters, God has a variety of ways that spell wealth and prosperity for us. Therefore, whoever has reverence for the Lord will obey these laws and implement them. To fear the Lord is to revere him in awe and be willing to heed to His wisdom and commandments. Wisdom is the application of knowledge and principles, which ultimately creates wealth for us, just as He did in King Solomon's case.

Proverbs 22:4 says: *"**By humility and the fear of the Lord are riches, and honor and life.**"* How sweet that sounds in the ears of believers! When humility and the fear of the Lord engulf us in our lives, we reap the rewards of riches, honor and life. These are the fundamental virtues every human being is striving for on Earth. By investing our trust in Him, we will get to know Him better so that we can rely solely on His providence. A God-fearing attitude unleashes a deep spiritual knowledge for us because true spiritual knowledge is only available to all those who "fear" the Lord. This is confirmed in **Proverbs 1:7,** which says: *"**The fear of the Lord is the beginning of knowledge; fools despise wisdom and instruction.**"*

Knowledge is not the sole spiritual gate that can be unlocked through the "fear of the Lord," but divine wisdom as well. **In Psalm 111:10,** the scriptures say that *"**the fear of the Lord is the beginning of wisdom; a good understanding have all those who do His commandments; His praise endures forever.**"* Job, the trustworthy man of God, confirms this in Job 28:28, by saying: *"**Behold the fear of the Lord, that is wisdom; and to depart from evil is understanding.**"* In this verse, the Bible is endorsing the "fear of the Lord" as not just an act of wisdom but even wisdom itself.

To cap it all, in **Isaiah 33:6,** it says: *"He will be the sure foundation for your times, a rich store of salvation and wisdom and knowledge; the fear of the Lord is the key to this treasure."* This verse makes it crystal clear that only the fear of the Lord opens the door to God's spiritual riches! Finally, a righteous and divine fear of the Lord displays itself through a life of humility and reverence to His will, purposes and commands. The benefits of such acts are enormous: wealth, long life and protection in all aspects of our lives.

YOU SEEK THE LORD IN ALL THINGS

"Thus, Hezekiah did throughout all Judah, and he did what was good and right and faithful before the Lord his God. And in every work that he began in the service of the house of God, in the law and in the commandment, to seek his God, he did it with all his heart. So he prospered."
2 Chronicles 31:20–21

The importance of seeking the Lord constantly and obeying His commandments as a means of guaranteeing our success and prosperity in life, cannot be overemphasized. Like consistency in being diligent in our work, seeking the Lord's guidance constantly also brings prosperity in its trail. Here we see Hezekiah blazing a trail of what we need to do constantly in our daily lives. He did what was good and served the Almighty with all his heart. The last verse tells us the outcome of such an attitude toward God. We are told that he prospered. Therefore, seeking the Lord daily in everything we do is a vital precept for success. If we look up to Him for all our needs, with faith, He will cause us to be prosperous, just as He prospered Hezekiah.

Psalm 1:1–3 says: *"Blessed is the man that walketh not in the counsel of the ungodly; nor standeth in the way of sinners, nor sitteth in the seat of the scornful. But his delight is in the law of the Lord; and in his law doth he meditate day and night. And he shall be like a tree planted by the rivers of water, that bringeth forth his fruit in his season; his leaf also shall not wither; and whatsoever he doeth shall prosper."* He who seeks the Lord has a strong passion for something precious, which is a delight in His laws and statutes. There are lots of things that block us from accessing God's blessings in our lives. Notable among them are factors elucidated in the verses above: joining hands with sinners and unbelievers, as well as being scornful and soliciting the advice of ungodly people. Such acts attract the disdain of the Almighty God, and we need to desist from that. However, inversely setting our hearts and minds on divine things brings blessings to us. We become constantly nourished with milk and honey, always fruitful and productive—and here comes the most amazing aspect that warms our hearts with joy: Whatever we do, prospers, because we seek His face constantly.

www.wisdomlaneofwealth.com

YOU ARE FAITHFUL AND PATIENT

"A faithful man will abound with blessings,
but he who hastens to be rich will not go unpunished."
Proverbs 28:20

This verse illustrates the fact that a faithful man who is truthful in his work, sticks to his promises and fulfills his contracts by complying with his obligations, abounds with blessings. It also emphasizes the fact that faithfulness is the key to God's blessings. Blessings come in different shapes and colors. There are common blessings such as the sunlight, moonlight and rain, and we do not need to be children of God to receive such blessings. The other type is described as unique blessings, which include both material and spiritual wealth. However, these types of blessings are available only to those who have strong faith in God as their provider.

There are a variety of ways we can demonstrate our faith in the Lord. Sometimes we are all compelled to wait and exercise patience, and waiting is a moment in time when our faithfulness is put to the test. Patience, we are told, is not the ability to wait but the ability to keep a good attitude while waiting. **Psalm 62:5 says:** *"My soul, wait thou only upon God, for my expectation is from Him."* If we are faithful, we will exercise patience and wait upon the Lord for providence. **Proverbs 13:11 says:** *"Dishonest money dwindles away, but whoever gathers money little by little makes it grow."* Here we see diligence, faithfulness and patience working together to ensure our prosperity. **John 15:7** assures us that God will bless us if we abide in His word: ***"If you remain in me and my words remain in you, ask whatever you wish, and it will be done for you."***

Our faithfulness should also be demonstrated in our finances. Our expenses should be planned with care, and we should also pay our tithes timely, remembering that everything we possess on Earth belongs to God. He is simply asking us to give one-tenth of our earnings back to Him as a test of our faith in His ability to sustain us financially, spiritually and physically. **Proverbs 3:9** urges us to ***"honor the Lord with your wealth and with the best part of everything you produce."*** If we are faithful enough in serving the Lord this way, we will definitely become wealthy if we apply His financial precepts as well.

The last half of **Proverbs 28:20,** cited above, gives us food for thought. If we want to acquire wealth hastily, we will ultimately be punished. The issue is that in every case, someone has to pay a price for our quick acquisition of wealth. The last portion of this verse states, ***"will not go unpunished."*** The idea that is inferred here is that some form of sin is committed that leaves us guilty—and will eventually lead to us being punished. God is strongly against those who make haste to acquire wealth, and cuts corners to do so. In other words, the Creator is not against people becoming wealthy. He did promise riches to the patriarchs, such as Abraham and Isaac, if they would follow Him with all their heart. Trusting the Lord faithfully with patience is a good sign that we will become wealthy.

www.wisdomlaneofwealth.com

YOU ARE HARDWORKING

"He who has a slack hand becomes poor, but the hand of the diligent makes rich." **Proverbs 10:4**

This scripture draws a sharp contrast between laziness and hard work. A person who is lazy invites poverty upon himself, whereas a hardworking person has a brighter hope of being successful in life. The Bible, therefore, advocates diligent work and strikes a warning note against laziness. Even before the fall of our first parents in the Garden of Eden, God gave Adam the responsibility to work. **Genesis 2:15 says:** *"The LORD God took the man and put him in the Garden of Eden to work and keep it."* To some, work is an unpleasant word. Here in this verse, we see that work existed before the fall. The fall itself just ensured that this work would be harder due to the sin Adam committed. But work is really good. The perspective of the holy scriptures on laziness is stern. It says: *"If anyone is not willing to work, let him not eat"* **(2 Thessalonians 3:10).** Hard work is a recipe for success in life.

The sluggard craves riches and attains nothing. **Proverbs 13:4 says:** *"The soul of the sluggard craves and gets nothing, while the soul of the diligent is richly supplied."* He prefers to play the Powerball lottery before attempting to pay his bills. He cherishes prosperity without making any effort to be productive. Laziness is recognized by refusal to initiate a job search. **Proverbs 26:13–14 says:** *"The slothful man saith, there is a lion in the way; a lion is in the streets. As the door turneth upon its hinges, so doth the slothful upon his bed."* Hard work

For bonuses go to ...

is God's basic principle of finance, and this explains why laziness and poverty go hand in hand. If we want to be wealthy, we must eschew laxity, because slackness is a recipe for financial ruin.

The coin spins in the opposite direction if we embrace diligence. In the vast majority of cases, our work ethic will determine our finances, and that is an important truth to know. There are no secrets to success because it is the result of hard work. More often than not, we get what we work for but not what we wish for. We might dream of success, but a dream does not materialize through magic; it takes hard work to become reality. As a matter of fact, there is no substitute for hard work when it comes to attaining a wealthy status. If we want to live for a meaningful purpose, then hard work is not an option; it becomes a necessity. The scriptures even consider slackness as a crime: **"Whoever is slack in his work is a brother to him who destroys" (Proverbs 18:9).**

A person who works hard is equipped with discipline, dedication and determination to achieve whatever he wants in life. Hard work is the foundation of any success. Nevertheless, hard work itself is worthless if we do not stay focused. Most of us start working hard, but somewhere along the line, we start neglecting consistency. We need to have a plan in place; otherwise, working hard aimlessly will be in vain. Having a strategy is always better than not having one. Success in life does not come by chance or luck as most people think. As a matter of fact, overnight prosperity is a total rarity, and it is sad to realize that it has turned into a goal for many. To step into the wisdom lane of wealth, we need to adopt a mentality of hard work.

www.wisdomlaneofwealth.com

YOU PRACTICE ABSTINENCE

"He who loves pleasure will be a poor man; he who loves wine and oil will not be rich."
Proverbs 21:17

The scripture cited above does not mince words about the relationship between pleasure lovers and poverty. The indulgence in womanizing is a sure ticket to the land of poverty. Lavishing money on women to solicit sensual pleasure drains our pockets of our hard-earned funds. The verse warns that those who love pleasure will ultimately become poor. More often than not, hard work, thriftiness and restraint are unknown vocabularies to such people. They only have vested interest in parties, pleasure and indulgence of their lust. Their focus is solely on enjoying themselves now, with little or no thought about the future.

The verse also mentions wine and oil as a warning to us. People who love both things will never become wealthy. The wine being mentioned here is not ordinary wine but the type that is very expensive and is obtained from expensive banquets. It is surprising to know that some wines cost as much as thousands of dollars, and someone who wants to impress his friends with an extraordinary banquet, does not mind buying the best of wines to serve them. The oils could also be very expensive in their price range; but for the rich, such ointments are offered to their guests as a sign of their wealth. As a result, their parties and banquets are filled with the smell of highly priced oils that cost a fortune. Spending huge sums of money on such things would lead up to the dwindling of one's wealth and ultimate poverty. **Proverbs 23:21** has this to say: ***"For drunkards and gluttons become poor, and drowsiness clothes them in rags."***

At the time of leaving his father's house, the prodigal son had great wealth, but he soon squandered it with a reckless and loose lifestyle. It is possible that the parties he organized for friends were legendary to those who attended them. However, one thing was certain about this reckless living, and that was the desertion of his so-called friends when he ran out of money. The Bible is warning us that those who love the pleasures of their flesh will not become wealthy. Their riches and prosperity will be consumed by their lust. The so-called stars in the entertainment and sporting world, and their broken lives, are the source of headlines of our newspapers and magazines. They are prime examples of people who love pleasure extremely. Stories are told of a famous boxer who squandered hundreds of millions of dollars on brand name cars with removable glass roofs, and he also spent about two million dollars on a bathtub. This famous sportsman's life ended so abysmally that he ended up filing for bankruptcy.

We should use our wealth wisely. The prudent man knows that the best way to invest his wealth is in celestial things that glorify God. He considers himself as an alien on this planet and knows that he will not take even a dime with him when he dies. We cannot become wealthy if we indulge ourselves in pleasure-seeking lifestyles that run parallel to divine principles.

YOU HAVE THIRST FOR KNOWLEDGE

"By knowledge, the rooms are filled with
all precious and pleasant riches."
Proverbs 24:4

This scripture indicates that knowledge is a key determinant of wealth, and every effort should be made to acquire it if we want to be prosperous. An inquisitive mind is always yearning for knowledge, because knowledge sharpens and refines our skills and ultimately makes us masters in our fields of specialization. As a matter of fact, the more we read, the more paradigm-shifting and mindset-upgrading lessons we grasp. Most successful people confirm that the more they learn (and apply that knowledge), the more income they earn, the more confident they feel, and the more financial freedom they create for themselves.

When we are open to learning new things, we are bound to be successful. We were all born with a blank mega brain that needs to be filled with knowledge. Knowledge of divine principles is guaranteed to make us prosperous. Principles are laws, and laws make us disciplined. The thirst for knowledge will motivate us to learn more divine principles that are geared toward making us wealthy. Knowledge permits us to think about issues and challenges from diverse perspectives, and a thirst for it ensures lifelong success.

The scriptures do not say that we are destroyed by lack of money. It states categorically that we are destroyed for lack of knowledge. **Hosea 4:6** says: *"My people are destroyed for lack of knowledge…."*

For bonuses go to ...

God has set in place laws, precepts and principles that govern prosperity in the universe. Whether we know them or not, they nevertheless govern every sphere of our lives. The sad aspect of it is that lack of knowledge does not change the way God's laws operate. However, it does keep us from obeying or benefiting from them. We are bound to suffer poverty and misery in any sphere of knowledge in which we lack knowledge, especially God's blueprint for financial freedom.

The key to the Creator's abundant life is knowledge; and ignorance stirs alienation from an abundant life of blessings and prosperity. Satan's tactical ploy is therefore apparent. He knows that only knowledge of God's precepts found in the Bible can usher us into the prosperity God intends for us to enjoy. Consequently, he uses every ploy at his disposal to keep us ignorant of the scriptures. We should never lose sight of the fact that God's wisdom and knowledge is what will bring us the wealth and prosperity we are seeking. When we have faith, He is capable of dropping wealth-generating ideas into our spirits, and by acting on those ideas, we will walk into the lane of wealth and prosperity.

YOU ARE FILLED WITH DIVINE WISDOM

"Happy is the man who finds wisdom, and the man who gains understanding; for her proceeds are better than the profits of silver, and her gain than fine gold. She is more precious than rubies, and all the things you may desire cannot compare with her. Length of days is in her right hand; in her left hand, riches and honor."
Proverbs 3:13–16

Wisdom is the application of divine laws and principles, and the main idea in this biblical verse is putting wisdom at the top of our list of whatever we intend to achieve in this life. It urges us to set our minds on wisdom and also pursue it at all costs. Here, God is inviting us to navigate our lives around the pursuit of wisdom. Biblically defined, wisdom is the ability to make divine choices. It is characterized by the fear of the Lord, which consists of trusting and relying solely on Him. The knowledge of laws and principles are the source of wisdom. The scriptures say, in **Proverbs 4:7: *"The beginning of wisdom is this: Get wisdom; though it cost all you have, get understanding."*** This verse is talking about the laws of God. You only become wise if you understand God's laws. Knowledge of laws produces boldness.

The ultimate goal of wisdom is to glorify God. Unfortunately, most people prefer to operate in conjunction with worldly wisdom, and the Bible depicts such people as "fools." A fool's source of wisdom originates from human minds through social media, magazines and worldly knowledge. But a wise man draws wisdom from divine principles enshrined in the word of God. Let us seek wisdom so that we can obtain all that God has purposed for us.

CHARITY AND GENEROSITY ARE YOUR STOCK IN TRADE

"One man gives freely, yet gains even more; another withholds unduly, but comes to poverty. A generous man will prosper; he who refreshes others will himself be refreshed."
Proverbs 11:24–25

Charity and generosity constitute an attitude of the heart; it is a way of living that stems out of thankfulness to the Creator for His grace and mercy. The way we give back to the needy in the society and for kingdom work is a form of worship to Him. It is not much about money than the posture we are displaying before God, who is the source of all things. When we share our wealth with others, we are paving the way for the Lord to use our resources to do His work on planet Earth. As the scripture quoted above affirms, generosity does not create a deficit. Paradoxically, it generates even more resources. **2 Corinthians 9:6–8** tells us: *"Whoever sows sparingly will also reap sparingly, and whoever sows generously will also reap generously. Each of you should give what you have decided in your heart to give, not reluctantly or under compulsion, for God loves a cheerful giver. And God is able to bless you abundantly, so that in all things at all times, having all that you need, you will abound in every good work."*

The scriptures speak very often about the poor and needy; it virtually commands us to give generously to the less fortunate and even advocate on their behalf. *"He who gives to the poor will lack nothing, but he who closes his eyes to them receives many curses"* **(Proverbs 28:27).** This is a powerful verse that confers prosperity on those who practice generosity. **Proverbs 11:25** minces no words when it says: *"A generous person will prosper; whoever refreshes others will be refreshed."* Let us be charitable and generous to the poor so that wealth and blessings of prosperity will flow our way eternally.

YOU ARE MEEK AND LIVE LIKE THE POOR

"One man pretends to be rich, yet has nothing; another pretends to be poor, yet has great wealth."
Proverbs 13:7

The meek are people filled with extreme humility. Their character is such that they do not need to prove their strength to others; they just demonstrate their quiet strength through their lifestyles. They are not restless with the obligation to find something to satisfy them more than what they already have. The Bible teaches us that it is the "meek" that will inherit the earth, and the meek are those who are resilient in putting their spirit under God's control. They find happiness in the knowledge that they are under the Creator's control, and the Lord actually rewards meekness but chastises arrogance. They are totally dependent on God and God alone.

In **Psalm 37:11**, David says: *"But the meek shall inherit the earth and shall delight themselves in the abundance of peace."* This verse gives us an insight into why meekness of character is visualized in biblical terms as a magnificent trait that needs to be emulated by all and sundry. The paradoxical power in meekness is seen in **Matthew 5:5**: *"Blessed are the meek, for they shall inherit the earth."* By this verse, Jesus is teaching us that "the way up is down." In other words, one must come low to go high! The meek keep a teachable spirit, so they love instructions and corrections. Prosperity stems from obeying divine principles of wealth creation, and principles guarantee success. Because the meek never stop learning, they empower themselves with divine wisdom. God says, in **Isaiah 29:19**, that *"the meek also shall increase their joy in the LORD."* Nothing beats a joyful relationship with God.

ASSOCIATION WITH HIGH ACHIEVING PEOPLE

"Walk with the wise and become wise,
or a companion of fools suffers harm."
Proverbs 13:20

High achievers are visionaries. They are ambitious, goal-oriented, wealth-minded and self-disciplined people, who are driven by a strong desire to achieve wealth and prosperity. As the scripture quoted above indicates, associating ourselves with high achievers will enable us to copy their lifestyle so that we too can become successful in life. Their character is worth emulating since they are avid goal setters and leave no stone unturned to achieve their aims and ambitions. They are a group of people who excel in terms of skill development and responsibilities. Any task they initiate, they make sure they wrap them up.

One major characteristic of high achievers is that they have a positive mindset. They see problems and setbacks as golden opportunities to pounce on and achieve success. The positive outlook they possess toward life assists them in overcoming any hurdles that crop up in their way, and they have the aptitude to stick to tasks until they are accomplished. **Proverbs 27:17** says: *"Iron sharpens iron, and one man sharpens another."* Associating ourselves with the wealthy will open golden doors of opportunity for us. Their zeal for prosperity will radiate hope and confidence in us to strive for success. All we need to do is listen to these high achievers and learn from them. **Proverbs 19:20** says: *"Listen to advice and accept discipline, and at the end you will be counted among the wise."* We can never go wrong financially when we associate ourselves with high achievers. We just need to be humble and teachable.

This is the law of people. To achieve success and prosperity, we need to protect ourselves from the wrong people. We must eliminate the wrong people from our lives. These are people who do not believe in our dreams and always try to blur our visions. They are all dream killers, and we need to weed them out of our lives. They aren't going anywhere, and they want you to stick with them. As the adage goes: "Birds of the same feather flock together." To the wise, a word is enough!

For bonuses go to www.wisdomlaneofwealth.com

W.I.N.K.

Chapter 6

Self-Destructive Thoughts About Wealth

LACK OF HIGH FORMAL EDUCATION

*"An intelligent heart acquires knowledge,
and the ear of the wise seeks knowledge."*
Proverbs 18:11

Most people feel that lack of higher academic achievements is a hindrance to attaining wealth. The ability to read and write is a must for all and sundry, since it is through literacy that knowledge of divine principles and laws can be attained. However, higher academic laurels are not necessarily prerequisites for attaining wealth. Billionaires like Bill Gates (Microsoft) and Steve Jobs (Apple) never attained PhDs, but they count among the wealthiest on planet Earth. This mentality for the achievement of prosperity is not divinely supported. In **Ecclesiastes 12:12**, the scriptures say: *"My son, beware of anything beyond these. Of making many books there is no end, and much study is a weariness of the flesh."* Solomon is most likely warning us to be careful about knowledge outside the scriptures. Knowledge of God's mandates for prosperity is the only key to prosperity.

For bonuses go to ...

We are commanded to "work," to be "fruitful," to "multiply" and to have "dominion" over all things. These are all business ideas we need to implement in our lives in order to be prosperous. Our gifts and talents are all inborn. We came with them at birth. God, our manufacturer, made sure we were equipped with every potential we need to be prosperous in life. This is why He gave Adam and Eve the mandate to be fruitful right from the word go. To be fruitful is to be productive. To be productive is to produce items such as food, products and services that solve human problems like hunger, thirst, communication, transportation, diseases, beauty, fashion, finances, legal issues, dental—and the list goes on and on. The purpose of higher education should solely be to refine our talents and skills so that we can gain expertise in our fields of specialization.

Psalm 139:14 says: ***"I will praise thee, for I am fearfully and wonderfully made: marvelous are thy works; and that my soul knoweth right well."*** To be fearfully and wonderfully made is a deep statement that connotes a lot of stuff. In Hebrew, to be wonderfully made is to be unique and set apart. It means we were created with a huge potential like our Creator, to create and co-create like our Mighty God. He created us in his own image, and that means he endowed us with incredible abilities that remain untapped. All we need to do is to discover our hidden potentials, refine them, become ourselves and serve society with our gifts. Businesses are born when we begin to solve problems facing mankind. So instead of worrying about higher formal education, let us worry about the hidden and untapped potentials that are buried within us. Every created being is blessed with a skill and a talent, and that is the reason our Creator commands us to be productive. Adam never attended any university, but God mandated him to be productive. The discovery of our skills and talents is the key to our success in life. We could be tailors, hairdressers, barbers, plumbers, dancers, song writers, authors, doctors, farmers, nutritionists, 100-meter runners, footballers, basketball players, tennis players, entertainers, fashion designers—and the list goes on and on. That is where our prosperity lies, not in master's degrees and PhDs.

BECOMING WEALTHY IS IMPOSSIBLE

*"I know that You can do all things,
and that no purpose of Yours can be thwarted."*
Job 42:2

It is hard to believe that what occupies our minds daily really affects our financial status. A vast majority of the masses feel they are unworthy of becoming rich, and that is a terrible blow to their mindset. God created us in his own image and gave us the potential to achieve anything we want on this planet. He commanded us to have dominion over everything, including the capacity to be wealthy. The scripture cited above confirms our ability to attain any goal we set before us, and that nothing can stop us from achieving our dreams.

While the ordinary man always hides in his cave of poverty and casts doubts about his potential to attain anything meaningful, the elites firmly believe in themselves and feel they deserve to be wealthy. They feel very confident about themselves and are always searching for ideas to solve problems facing humanity. And because they have such strong beliefs about themselves, their behavior always draws them closer to the materialization of their dreams. But that is not the case for the masses. The cultural mindset they have inherited bars them from believing in their capabilities. They have allowed society to define who they are, so they find it extremely difficult to extricate themselves from such devastating mindsets. They allow the opinions of other people to define them and dictate to them what they can and cannot do. That is why they are always caught up in the sea of sameness. Consequently, they end up acquiring a natural aversion to prosperity.

Till such time that we cast aside our inferiority complexes, we will always be poor shadows of our original selves. We need to brush aside our feelings of inadequacy regarding our self-worth and stop measuring ourselves against other people's standards. We lose our self-identity by doing so, and that compels us to have a very poor self-concept. There is nothing we cannot achieve if we gear all our efforts toward a well-defined goal. God gave each human being gifts and skills that need to be tapped to ensure our prosperity. It therefore behooves us to discover our gifts and talents and pursue them relentlessly. We should never bow down to the accolades the world brands us with, since they are all dream killers. Never should we lose guard of our self-esteem. **Proverbs 23:18** says: *"There is surely a future hope for you, and your hope will not be cut off."* All we need to do is believe in our potential to achieve success.

If we continue to be trapped in the culture of nothingness, we will never be able to enter the wisdom lane of wealth. Our potential is so great that we should not allow others to express their opinions on who we are and what we are capable of doing to amass wealth the right way. God has designed us for prosperity.

THERE IS NO MONEY TO MAKE MONEY

The ordinary person believes that one needs to have one's own money to invest before one can become wealthy. This viewpoint betrays ignorance of a lucrative method of acquiring wealth. There is a system called OPM, which is an acronym for "other people's money." The accurate financial term used to describe this method is "leveraging," and it is one of the secrets of the rich. It may be as simple as approaching friends and family members or a bank. By providing a business plan and discussing a payback plan, we can borrow a certain amount of money to start a business of our own. The credit score system creates a golden opportunity for us to obtain loans at reasonable interest rates from the banks. All we need is an excellent score backed by a solid job employment record.

Using other people's money to make money is exemplified by almost everyone who has a mortgage on his house. The banks lend us money to buy a home with an amortization that sometimes spans up to forty years. As we pay our monthly mortgages over the years, we build solid equity in the value of our homes, which can be cashed out after selling them or even be taken out to purchase other houses. What is happening here is that we are unconsciously using the banks' money to make more money. Sometimes we could also take investment loans from the banks and invest them. This highlights the importance of maintaining good credit scores. We need to be creditworthy in order to have access to such financial privileges.

LOTTERIES AND GAMBLING

"Wealth gained hastily will dwindle,
but whoever gathers little by little will increase."
Proverbs 13:11

Lots of people believe that winning a lottery is the only way to become wealthy. Some have become so addicted to it that not a single week passes by without them buying lottery tickets or going to the casino to gamble. They are lured into playing the lottery with promises that their lives will scale up if they could just hit the jackpot. To gamble is to risk a valuable item on an outcome that depends on chance. Since the outcome of a lottery depends on chance, and indulging in it consists of risk, the definition then taints lottery as gambling. The scripture cited above cautions us against the indulgence in quick schemes of making money. The fact is, get-rich-quick schemes entice us from trusting God as the real source of our financial security. In **Proverbs 28:20,** it says: *"A faithful man will be richly blessed, but one eager to get rich will not go unpunished."* First of all, the odds of winning are so slim that we might as well throw our money into the garbage bin. As stewards of God, not a dime that comes into our wallets belongs to us. God owns everything, and we need to manage our resources well.

Indulgence in lotteries and gambling makes us lazy and unproductive because it divests us of a working mindset. It is like sitting idle and expecting miracles from God. A time came when some Pharisees and Sadducees went to Jesus and asked for a miracle to prove who He was. The answer Jesus gave was this: *"An evil and adulterous generation seeks after a sign, and a sign will not be given it, except the sign of Jonah"* **(Matthew 16:4).** This is an indication that gambling and lotteries are somehow evil. Now, some may ask whether buying stocks can be equated to buying lottery tickets. My answer to that is no, because in the stock market, we actually own shares of the companies that we invest in. We are therefore purchasing valuable stuff in the stock market that will gain more currency one day.

The risk involved in lotteries or gambling is when we put the upkeep of our families on the line and are not capable of affording meals or paying our bills. We end up leading lives of debauchery by indulging in drunkenness and drug abuse. Statistics indicate that about 70% of people who suddenly receive a windfall of cash through a lottery, lose everything in a few years. This proves what the Creator says in **Proverbs 13:11.** It is incredible to hear of a man who won $21 million dollars in 2001 and lost it all by 2006! *"Cast but a glance at riches and they are gone"* **(Proverbs 23:5).** The fact is, the Creator wants us to earn our money through honest means by working hard. **2 Thessalonians 3:10** says: *"The one who is unwilling to work shall not eat."*

As stewards of God, I do not think we should indulge in lotteries, because the Bible teaches that when we work, we provide service to mankind. **Ephesians 4:28** says: *"Anyone who has been stealing must*

For bonuses go to ...

steal no longer, but must work, doing something useful with their own hands, that they may have something to share." I am convinced beyond reasonable doubts that gambling is smeared with greediness. Playing the lottery goes against work ethics. When we work, we invest our labor for the benefit of mankind, and we get paid too. There is a mutual profit that occurs. In a lottery, only one person wins, and everybody else loses. We cannot depend on chance to become wealthy and prosperous, so lotteries should not feature in our plans for success in life. Playing the lottery is closely tied to an addictive nature in our lives, which is not pleasing to our Creator. The sad aspect of it all is that it is the marginalized poor that engage heavily in playing the lottery, and the discretionary amount of money they have at their disposal, they waste it on a windfall that promises unrealistic hopes.

W.I.N.K.

Chapter 7

How We Lose Money Despite Hard Work

NON-PAYMENT OF TITHES AND OFFERINGS

"Will a man rob God? Yet ye have robbed me.
But ye say, wherein have we robbed thee?
In tithes and offerings."
Malachi 3:8

Tithes and offerings are God's financial management program for mankind. As stewards of the Creator, we are mere managers of the resources He has put at our disposal. We own nothing on Earth: *"For naked we came, naked we shall go."* The reason I brand tithes and offerings as God's financial management program is that **Malachi 3:10** says: *"Bring the whole tithe into the storehouse, that there may be food in my house. Test me in this, says the Lord Almighty, and see if I will not throw open the floodgates of heaven and pour out so much blessings that there will not be room enough to store it."* All that the Lord requires from us is a tenth of our incomes. To avoid digging holes in our pockets, we need to pay our tithes and offerings. **Verse 11 of Malachi 3** says: *"I will prevent pests from devouring your crops, and the vines in your fields will not drop their fruit before it is ripe."* He may not send pests to us since we do not grow crops, but we will always find ourselves with debts and other irrelevant expenses if we violate His mandate of paying tithes and offerings. Prevention of pests also alludes to sickness and diseases. God's blessings come in a variety of ways.

Till such time that we grasp fully the concept of God's ownership of all resources, we will never understand the importance of giving tithes and offerings. *"The earth is the Lord's, and the fullness thereof, the world, and they that dwell therein. For He hath founded it upon the seas and established it …* **(Psalm 24:1–3).** Most of the time, we feel we acquired wealth through our own strength, but **Deuteronomy 8:18** says: *"But remember the Lord your God, for it is He who gives you the ability to produce wealth."* When we pay our tithes and offerings, God does not rain money on our roofs as some believe. Rather, He gives us the ability to get wisdom, intelligence, concepts, schemes and ideas to make more money. **Proverbs 3:9** says: *"Honor the Lord with your wealth…."* Any wealth, talent, gift, power or strength we possess has its roots in God. Even our ability to give generously toward the kingdom work originates from God. This explains even more how King David was able to offer all the treasure he had acquired, to the Lord, with ease. The idea that God owns everything is not just a matter of faith. It is a fact, which we will take cognizance of and incorporate into our worldview or discard our own destruction.

Offerings are the seeds for our next harvest, and we reap what we sow. In **2 Corinthians 9:6,** it says: *"Remember this: Whoever sows sparingly will also reap sparingly; and whoever sows generously will also reap generously."* God's generosity is immeasurable, and since He created us in His own image, we need to be generous when it comes to giving for the propagation of His word. If we refuse to pay our tithes and offerings, we are merely inviting curses of poverty and illness upon ourselves. **Malachi 3:9** says: *"You are cursed with a curse, for you are robbing me, the whole nation of you."*

GREED

"The righteousness of the upright will deliver them, but the treacherous will be caught by their own greed."
Proverbs 11:6

Though the Bible instructs us on how to acquire wealth, it also cautions us on the variety of ways through which holes can be dug ironically in our pockets to make us lose money at lightning speed. One of the mainstream pitfalls is greed. Due to laziness and our apathy toward work, we are often inclined to want to get rich quickly and with ease. Greed compels us to reach out for extra, and by doing so, we end up losing what we have in expectation of gaining more than what we should hope for. **Proverbs 28:22** says: *"A man with an evil eye hastens after wealth, and does not know that want will come upon him."*

Greed causes us to see nothing but personal gains, which often culminates in depriving us of compassion for others. It is really the mismanagement of resources for personal benefits. A greedy person will manipulate resources so that he or she becomes the ultimate beneficiary alone. No wonder it is one of the seven deadly sins the Bible talks about. **Jeremiah 6:13** says: *"From the least to the greatest,*

For bonuses go to ...

all are greedy for gain; prophets and priests alike, all practice deceits." Because of its spiritually cancerous nature, Jesus warned us about it in **Luke 12:15:** *"**Be on your guard against all kinds of greed; life does not consist in an abundance of possessions.**"* We must learn to be happy with whatever we have. **1 Timothy 6:6** says: *"**But godliness with contentment is great gain.**"* Greed is an ugly sin, and the term cannot be used in any way that is not deplorable. It can dig holes in our pockets and impoverish us in a variety of ways.

Since we want it all for our own selves, we tend to look at all those things we could have that present life as being even better. We look at bigger houses with huge decks and patios, as well as flashy cars and extra-large, flat-screen televisions. Unfortunately, all those expenses have to be paid, and it can lead to devastating credit card debts, loans we can never pay back and the eventual loss of everything in order to pay back our creditors. Subsequently, the things we thought we owned, end up owning us. When greed creeps into our lives, we tend to indulge in excesses: more wine, more junk food and more of everything, creating all kinds of illnesses for us.

Thirdly, greed can make us break laws by doing some weird things. It is incredible to hear of high government officials who use their diplomatic positions to deal in drugs. They get caught and imprisoned, thus ending their careers in ruins. Cheating on taxes for a few dollars constitutes a federal offense that can lead us to imprisonment. The zeal to have more and more can lead us to gamble away all our resources. Gambling does bring riches to some people, but for the vast majority of us, it is a losing game. Greed, when combined with gambling, creates a recipe for poverty. Gambling is a serious addiction, and greed is at its roots. We want more, and that is why we gamble; so in an attempt to win back all that we lose, we end up losing everything.

This is why the Bible cautions us to be very careful about greed. **Proverbs 1:19** says: *"So are the ways of everyone who is greedy for gain. It takes away the life of its owners."* Greed is deadly and has the capacity to wreak financial havoc on us.

LAZINESS

"I passed by the field of the sluggard,
and by the vineyard of the man lacking sense; and behold,
it was completely overgrown with thistles. Its surfaces were
covered with nettles, and its stone wall was broken down."
Proverbs 24:30–31

One tragic way we lose money or dig holes in our pockets is through laziness. In the scripture quoted above, the sluggard not only declines efforts to obtain wealth because of his laziness, he likewise neglects to capitalize on the resources he has. In other words, we are encouraged not to reject or underestimate what we already own. Now, who is a sluggard? A sluggard is a lazy person and is always hinged to his bed. Sluggards' stock in trade is procrastination. They never get anything done on time. That is why the Creator loathes laziness. The Bible rings bells of danger regarding the ways of the

For bonuses go to ...

sluggard: *"A little sleep, a little slumber, a little folding of the arms to rest, and poverty will come upon you like a robber, and want like an armed man"* **(Proverbs 6:10)**.

Right from creation, work has been God's prescription for poverty. He created us in his own image, and we see Him working every day till the seventh day when He rested from His works. Thus, He set an example for us to follow suit. In **Genesis 1:28,** it says: *"And God blessed them; and God said unto them: Be fruitful and multiply, and replenish the earth, and subdue it; and have dominion over the fish and the sea."* Apart from bringing forth children, with their children also bringing forth children, and managing the entire earth, this commandment of God is also pregnant with business ideas of producing abundantly and having dominion over the products we produce. So, man was actually created to work like the Creator. That is why the scripture says: *"Whoever is lazy regarding his work is also a brother to the master of destruction"* **(Proverbs 18:9).** Such is the lens through which God views laziness.

A quick glance at the sluggard's vineyard, as quoted above, tells all about his attitude to life. He is able-bodied, has not gone out on a trip but he does not care a fig about the thorns that have invaded his residence. He is so drowned in apathy that nothing compels him to tidy up his yard. What a dangerous lifestyle it is to be a sluggard! **Proverbs 13:4** says: *"The soul of the sluggard craves and gets nothing, while the soul of the diligent is richly supplied."* This is a showcase of how laziness can plunge us into poverty. To step into the wisdom lane of wealth, we need to shun laziness and embrace hard work. The Bible admonishes us: *"Go to the ant, thou sluggard, consider her ways, and be wise: Which having no guide, overseer or ruler, provideth her meat in the summer and gathereth her food in the harvest"* **(Proverbs 6:6–8).** The ant is a diligent creature. It is small but very prudent in its ability to optimize its time, skills and resources. That is exactly what God wants us to do. Time is a precious currency and, as a result, we need to reject procrastination and make profitable use of our time in acquiring wealth for the glory of God. *"Any who do not provide for their relatives, and especially for their own household, has denied the faith and is worse than an unbeliever"* (1Timothy 5:8).

WRONG RELATIONSHIPS
"For a prostitute is like a deep pit; a harlot is like a narrow well. Indeed, she lies in wait like a robber, and increases the unfaithful among men."
Proverbs 23:27–28

It goes without saying that a licentious life is a sure way of drowning in the sea of poverty. Prostitution is one of the ancient forms of illicit gain in the world, and the Bible cautions us to stay away from prostitutes if we do not want any holes in our pocket. *"Now then, my sons, listen to me, and do not depart from the words of my mouth. Keep your way far from her (the prostitute) and do not go near the door of her house, lest you give your vigor to others, and your years to the cruel one; lest strangers be filled with your strength, and your hard-earned goods go to the house of an alien"* (Proverbs 5:7–10).

For bonuses go to ...

These verses are strong indicators of how a promiscuous life filled with unprincipled sexual lust can impoverish us and drain our energies at the same time.

Friendship is the Lord's special gift to us, and without companionship, life becomes boring and lonely. However, not all friendships are worthy of our time; some are worth sacrificing to keep, but others lead to regret, sorrow and poverty. ***"Do not be with heavy drinkers of wine, or with gluttonous eaters of meat; for the heavy drinker and glutton will come to poverty, and drowsiness will clothe a man with rags"* (Proverbs 23:20–21).** Lots of money has been wasted as a result of a reckless choice of relationships. The scriptures warn us that courting friendships with the wrong people would land us in a pit of poverty. It is obvious that the world harbors great thoughts about wine, ladies and music. We find admonition in Proverbs that we should opt for spiritual music that can fill us with words of wisdom.

It takes wisdom to identify which friendships to keep and which to discard. We will be spared a great deal of trouble if we make this decision as quickly as possible. I am glad to say that the Bible gives a life-changing insight on the choice of friendships. Biblically, a good friend is someone who is selfless and always seeks our best interest. **Proverbs 18:24** says: *"A man who has friends must himself be friendly, but there is a friend who sticks closer than a brother."* In contrast, there are toxic friends as well. These types of friends are selfish, ungrateful and self-centered. Such friends are totally dependent on us and receptive all the time. They keep their resources to themselves and are never willing to give in return. No wonder they shun our company in times of crisis, since they can no longer milk us. These are the types of friends we should avoid. They would stab us in the back at any given time, indicating how treacherous they are.

Proverbs advises us to *"walk with the wise and become wise, for a companion of fools suffers harm"* **(Proverbs 13:20).** Some of the harmful effects of such friendships are depletion of our financial resources and loss of our identity as righteous people, since bad company also corrupts good manners.

EXTRAVAGANT LIFE

"There is precious treasure and oil in the dwelling of the wise, but a foolish man swallows it up."
Proverbs 21:20

No matter how much wealth we acquire, if we begin to lead an extravagant life, holes will definitely be dug in our pockets. When we are extravagant, we spend more money than we can afford. The adage says that *"a fool and his money are soon parted."* This indicates that one of the ways fools are separated from their possessions is to spend extraordinarily and save too little. They are never happy with the least of anything, so they go on a spending spree till their coffers become empty. This explains even more why the scriptures advise us as follows: *"Have you found honey? Eat only what you need, lest you have it in excess and vomit it"* **(Proverbs 25:16).**

Proverbs 21:17 says: *"He that loveth pleasure shall be a poor man: he that loveth wine and oil shall not be rich."* An affinity for pleasure is a prime example of how we dig holes in our pockets when we are wealthy. A poor man knows the real value of money and will not dare waste it, but a wealthy man is highly extravagant and is always seeking a chance to spend and lose money. By indulging in extravagance, we act like fools and feel like fools, but we still enjoy it unconsciously. So, we can infer from this that extravagance is the pitfall of the rich and wealthy. An adage says that *"a miser grows rich by looking poor, but an extravagant man grows poor by masquerading himself as rich."*

ACTING AS A SURETY

"A man lacking in sense pledges and becomes surety in the presence of his neighbor."
Proverbs 17:18

When we act as surety for people, we run the risk of being in a financial mess, and the scriptures warn us against that. We should not count ourselves among those who give pledges and become sureties for debts. Volunteering surety for a neighbor is the process whereby we assume responsibility for their debts. The Bible deems such acts as foolish—*"a man lacking in sense"*—and it is so risky that we are cautioned to resolve the situation immediately. *"So do this, my son, to free yourself, since you have fallen into your neighbor's hands: Go to the point of exhaustion, and give your neighbor no rest."* In one way or the other, we tend to immerse ourselves in a vulnerable situation; we become a victim of the one for whom we have become surety. *"You have been trapped by what you said, ensnared by the words of your mouth"* (Proverbs 6:2).

The dangers of being a surety for someone are not farfetched. Acting as a surety for a person whose character and financial honesty are unspecified puts us at risk of financial ruin. We may ultimately find ourselves in a state of not having the means to cover the debts involved and end up losing even our own bed. **Proverbs 22:27** says: *"If you lack the means to pay, your very bed will be snatched from under you."* We have to be very smart because the mere fact that the person needs us to become a surety for him, already indicates that he or she is of unproven financial character. In short, acting as sureties can be compared to the act of gambling, because we may lose heavily if the one we are trying to help defaults on his payments. Secondly, the fact that we are sureties may inversely inspire recklessness on the person's part. After all, if he is not capable of paying his debts, the surety will have to step into his shoes and pay for him.

In conclusion, the warnings that the scriptures are giving us are in conjunction with being sureties for strangers. However, when we co-sign an application with a son or daughter, it enables them to build their own credit status. As parents, we must be on our guard to the risk of instructing our children to be irresponsible by always rallying to their rescue financially. Promising others that we will always act as sureties for their financial woes, especially when it is due to their own folly, just encourages financial irresponsibility. It might be for a specific amount for the purchase of a vehicle or a home, which would serve as collateral. We are cautioned about being extremely generous to

For bonuses go to ...

people we scarcely know. We struggle to pay our own bills, so we should not court problems by assuming the liabilities of strangers. Alternatives exist for handling the needs of those who request us to act as sureties. Making personal loans to them, backed by an assurance of repayment in the form of a collateral asset, would be appropriate. The basic advice can be summed up like this: avoid guaranteeing people's debts.

www.wisdomlaneofwealth.com

W.I.N.K.

Chapter 8

Miseries of Wealth Without God

PRIDE AND ARROGANCE

"The rich are wise in their own eyes; one who is poor and discerning sees how deluded they are."
Proverbs 28:11

At its core, pride is putting ourselves in the place of God. First of all, it indicates our reluctance to depend on Him, and an attempt to be self-sufficient. Secondly, arrogance is the refusal to give Him the glory He deserves, and to seek glory for ourselves instead. Even though we may gain our wealth through godly and righteous means, we are still prone to potential dangers that may put us at risk of losing our faith in God. Wealth can lead us to the brink of pride and arrogance. It is easy to ascribe our prosperity to our own ability, cleverness or hard work. But scriptures warn us never to say: *"The power and strength of my hands have made this wealth for me"* **(Deuteronomy 8:17).** It is God who gives us life and the ability to acquire wealth.

Pride is the root cause of so many sins; having the means to afford everything puts us in danger. We easily fall prey to arrogance, with no regard for ethical values. **Proverbs 15:25** says: *"The Lord tears down* the proud man's house but he keeps the widow's boundaries intact." This worsens our case when pride invades our thoughts because of our prosperity. We are really working against God when we act in arrogance and seek to glorify ourselves. Rolling in wealth, we are headed toward destruction because the choices we make in life have more to do with our pride and convincing ourselves and others that we matter, than they do with honoring God.

We can acquire wealth, but we need to rid ourselves of pride because we worship a Savior who is humble. Therefore, to ward off arrogance, **Philippians 2:3; 6–8** advises us: *"Do nothing out of selfish ambition or vain conceit, but in humility consider others better than ourselves. Your attitude should be the same as that of Christ Jesus: who, being in very nature God, did not consider equality with God something to be grasped, but made Himself nothing, taking the very nature of a servant, being made in human likeness. And being found in appearance as a man, He humbled Himself and became obedient to death—even death on the cross!"*

Finally, all that we should concern ourselves with, when we become prosperous, is to be humble and not attribute our prosperity to our own power and might, as the Bible teaches us. We should use our wealth to glorify our Creator. Pride is a spiritual cancer that needs to be avoided. **Proverbs 11:2** says: *"When pride comes, then comes disgrace, but with humility comes wisdom."* It was pride that turned an angel into a devil (Lucifer). And **Proverbs 16:5** says: *"The LORD detests all the proud of heart. Be sure of this: They will not go unpunished."* Lastly, **Proverbs 16:18** says: *"Pride goes before destruction, a haughty spirit before a fall."* Such miseries associated with wealth can be avoided if we stick to divine principles regarding wealth and prosperity.

FALSE SENSE OF SECURITY

"Ephraim boasts, 'I am very rich; I have become wealthy. With all my wealth, they will not find in me any iniquity or sin.'"
Hosea 12:8

The acquisition of wealth often leads us to feel self-sufficient, complacent and a false sense of security. A classic example of this is Ephraim's boast as cited above. Later in **Hosea 13:6**, a description of Israel's rejection of God is pitiful: *"When I fed them, they were satisfied; they were satisfied, and their heart was proud."*

Jesus also comments on the dangers of wealth lulling us into a false sense of security, in his parable of the rich fool. This reflects the stupidity of placing extreme importance on wealth. The point of this parable is that we should not devote our lives to the gathering and accumulation of wealth. God says to the man in the story, "And the things you have prepared, whose will they be?" This echoes the thought expressed in **Ecclesiastes 2:18:** *"I hated all my toil in which I toil under the sun, seeing that I must leave it to the man who will come after me."* You see it all the time in people who are mainly devoted to the accumulation of wealth. What happens to all that wealth when they die? It gets left behind to others who didn't earn it and won't appreciate it. Furthermore, if money is your master, that means God is not **(Matthew 6:24).**

For bonuses go to ...

The second point of the parable of the rich fool is the fact that we are not blessed by God to hoard our wealth to ourselves. We are blessed to be a blessing in the lives of others, and we are blessed to build the kingdom of God. The Bible says: ***"If our riches increase, we are not to set our hearts upon them"* (Psalm 62:10).** The Bible also says there is ***"one who gives freely and grows all the richer"* (Proverbs 11:24).** Finally, the Bible says that ***"we are to honor God with the first fruits of our increase"* (Proverbs 3:9–10).** The point is clear: If we honor God with what He has given us, He will bless us with more so that we can honor Him with more. There is a passage in **2 Corinthians 9:6–15** that summarizes this aptly. In that passage, Paul says: ***"And God is able to provide you with every blessing in abundance, so that having all contentment in all things at all times, you may abound in every good work."*** We are blessed by God, so we can in turn ***"abound in every good work"*** and be a blessing in the lives of others. So, if God has blessed you with material wealth, "set not your heart on it," and "be rich toward God." That is the message of the parable of the rich fool.

It is only too easy to think that we have no need of God when our bellies are full, life is good and the future seems assured.

www.wisdomlaneofwealth.com

OBSESSION WITH OUR OWN NEEDS

"Let each of you look not only to his own interests, but also to the interests of others."
Philippians 2:4

Prosperity can likewise render us less responsive to other people's needs, thus draining us of compassion and mercy. The parable of the rich man and Lazarus in **Luke 16:19–31,** illustrates this point. Even though the poor man, Lazarus, lives in great distress at the rich man's gate, the rich man is impervious to his plight, so consumed is he with his own lifestyle and consumption. It is not a sin to be wealthy, but the rich man's sin was that he was pretty happy with his wealth without God. His life was the type in which he had no need. He never thought of Lazarus or cared about him. He might have been laid at the rich man's gate or porch because he was poverty-stricken and had no resources for any medical help. And most probably, those who left him at the porch had hoped that the rich man would help him since he was so richly blessed by God. Sadly enough, he was so engrossed in his riches that he felt Lazarus should suffer for being poor. Ironically, even in Hades, the rich man is obsessed with his own needs and still views Lazarus as nothing but a pawn. Based on the advice quoted in the scripture above, we need to seek the interests of others as well, not only ours.

"If anyone has material possessions and sees a brother or sister in need but has no pity on them, how can the love of God be in that person?" **(1 John 3:17)** This should be a shocking revelation to us. It underlies the danger of immersing ourselves in selfishness. Wealth is

a blessing from God and, as such, it is meant to change lives around us.

ENSLAVEMENT OF OUR HEARTS

"... if riches increase, do not set your heart on them."
Psalm 62:10

The most seductive of all the dangers is the lure riches have in capturing our hearts and dividing our loyalties. Here we see the scripture's acknowledgement of the power that money wields. The Psalmist warns us of this when he writes: ***"If riches increase, do not set your heart on them."***

The danger is also spelled out in **Deuteronomy 8:12–17**: ***"When you have eaten your fill and have built fine houses and live in them; and when your herds and flocks have multiplied, and your silver and gold is multiplied ... then do not exalt yourself, forgetting the Lord your God ... Do not say to yourself, 'My power and the might of my own hand have gotten me this wealth.'"*** These are sobering words. Perhaps this is why the writer of **Proverbs 30:8-9** asks God: ***"Give me neither poverty nor riches; feed me with the food that I need, or I shall be full, and deny you, and say, "Who is the Lord?" or I shall be poor, and steal, and profane the name of my God."***

The dangers of wealth are even more pronounced in the New Testament; central to the attitude of Jesus is his statement: ***"No one can serve two masters; for a slave will either hate the one and love*** *the other or be devoted to the one and despise the other. You cannot serve God and wealth"* **(Matthew 6:24).** The word used here for wealth is mammon. Some translations, such as the NIV, capitalize this word to emphasize that Jesus is pitting one God against another. Both seek our allegiance and worship. Wealth is not neutral. It's insatiable—once you have some of it, you seem to keep wanting more and more of it. No wonder Jesus commented to his disciples after his encounter with the rich young man: *"Truly I tell you; it will be hard for a rich person to enter the kingdom of heaven. Again, I tell you, it is easier for a camel to go through the eye of a needle than for someone who is rich to enter the kingdom of God"* **(Matthew 19:23–24).** For Jesus then, wealth is a dangerous thing. It is like a stick of dynamite—having the potential to do much good but also to cause a lot of damage. And the more you have, the greater the risks.

WEALTH BREEDS GREEDINESS

*"Whoever loves money never has enough;
whoever loves wealth is never satisfied with their income.
This too is meaningless."*
Ecclesiastes 5:10

Simply defined, greed is the insatiable desire to have more possessions and money in order to feed our egos. Greed is the attitude that is never quite satisfied and keeps saying, "I want a little bit more." Gaining provision and wealth may fuel dissatisfaction with what we have and, with it, the desire for more. Envy and covetousness can easily develop as we compare our lot with that of others who have more than we have. In fact, the drive to accumulate and to consume more makes us vulnerable to manipulation.

We easily find ourselves perpetually desiring more. We have trained our appetites to always desire more. Working out what is enough is exceptionally challenging within this environment. Perhaps this is what James was addressing when he wrote: *"You covet something and cannot obtain it, so you engage in disputes and conflicts. You do not have, because you do not ask. You ask and do not receive, because you ask wrongly, in order to spend what you get on your pleasures"* **(James 4:2–3).**

The strongest warning against greediness is found in **Luke 12:15,** which says: *"Then He said to them, 'Watch out! Be on your guard against all kinds of greed; life does not consist in the abundance of possessions.'"* When the Lord blesses us with wealth, we need to exercise extra caution in order not to be swept into the currents of greed. No wonder it is counted among the seven deadly sins that the Lord hates. **Proverbs 6:16–19** says: *"These six things doth the LORD hate: yea, seven are an abomination unto him …."* So, greed is a dangerous sin that needs to be avoided, but wealth is a serious responsibility to be generous to the needy. Paul states that greed is equivalent to idolatry and attracts the anger of God. In **Colossians 3:5,** the Bible says: *"So put to death whatever in your nature belongs to the earth; sexual immorality, impurity, shameful passion, evil desire, and greed which is idolatry."* Paul warns further, in **1 Corinthians 6:9–10,** that the greedy will not inherit the kingdom of God. In **verse 10,** it says: *"Thieves, the greedy, drunkards, the verbally abusive, and swindlers will not inherit the kingdom of God."*

However, this danger associated with wealth does not mean that we should take a vow of abject poverty and liquidate all our possessions. Wealth has a divine role to play in our lives on Earth. As stated earlier on, we are blessed to be a blessing to others! There are a bunch of triggers that should signal to us that we are treading the path of greediness. One of them is viewing our wealth as ours. The minute we believe that our strength and abilities are the sources of our prosperity, we cross the divine lines. Secondly, the instant we feel more concerned about making money and acquiring other assets than about our eternal salvation and destiny, we fall an easy prey to the spirit of greediness. Finally, if we feel drawn to easy and quick schemes of building wealth, then we are swimming in the sea of greediness. This includes, but is not limited to, gambling and engaging in lotteries. Let us ward off greed when the Lord blesses us with wealth.

WEALTH CAN FILL US WITH ANXIETY

We can become anxious and full of worry about the future provision of our needs. One would think that this kind of concern would only fill the hearts and minds of those who genuinely don't have enough. However, most people who have plenty also develop this subtle stress. Having more than the basic necessities seems to make us more anxious because now we have more stuff to worry about losing. The fear of not having enough is what drives some people to work unnecessarily long hours, under the pretext that to provide for their children means buying them the latest gadgets and fashionable clothes, when what they really need most is the parents' time and attention. Others are consumed by the fear that they won't

For bonuses go to ...

have enough money to sustain them through their twilight years. And so they plan for their future provision at the cost of serving God and others in the here and now, developing rich and meaningful relationships or living a balanced life.

Still others lie awake at night worrying about whether a particular investment is safe, or dreaming of how to get the house or car they really want. In fact, more anxious energy is consumed on money matters than on almost anything else. Is it this anxiety that drives people to do things they normally wouldn't—like commit fraud, be less than honest, sacrifice a friendship or compromise their values? Having more than the basic provisions we need can be a burden. The well-known words of Jesus, in **Matthew 6**—spoken to a crowd who knew what it was like to struggle to make ends meet—are particularly important: *"Do not worry, saying, 'What will we eat?' or 'What will we drink?' or 'What will we wear?' For it is the Gentiles who strive for all these things; and indeed your heavenly Father knows that you need all these things. But strive first for the kingdom of God and his righteousness, and all these things will be given to you as well"* **(Matthew 6:31–33).** This is a very provocative statement of Jesus. It is not easy to trust God—particularly if your economic future is uncertain. However, we need to exercise faith in the Lord. When Jesus urged his followers not to worry about tomorrow, we must assume he led them by example. If we ask, "Can anyone really trust God this way?" we can answer that at least one person did. **1 Peter 5:7** encourages us to cast all our anxieties on the Lord because He cares.

W.I.N.K.

Chapter 9

Divine Attitudes Toward Wealth

STEWARDSHIP

"The earth is the Lord's and all that is in it."
Psalm 24:1

Wealth achievement behooves us to nurture biblical attitudes, which will enable us to act in consonance with the precepts of God. The first fundamental attitude the Bible harps on is stewardship. The first humans were directed by God to take care of the Garden and all creatures and plants within it. This is often called the "creation mandate." God shared the day-to-day management of the Garden with Adam and Eve. They were to view themselves as caretakers of the created order. This trusteeship was built on the principle that ultimate ownership of everything we have and inhabit is not ours but God's. God is the owner, who has entrusted management to us, to be exercised according to his purposes. As the Psalmist declares, *"The earth is the Lord's and all that is in it"* **(Psalm 24:1)**. King David affirmed the same in his prayer in front of the people of Israel, at the establishment of the Temple building fund. *"All things come from you, and of your own have we given"* **(1 Chronicles 29:14)**.

For bonuses go to ...

We have no right to claim absolute ownership of any of our resources; neither money, possessions, businesses, abilities, physical environments nor heritage. We are merely trustees of whatever provision or wealth we receive. Fiduciary duty, or stewardship, is a key element of trusteeship. While trustees are given a great deal of freedom to act and make decisions regarding resource allocation, they do so on behalf of the true owners or beneficiaries of the body they manage. And, of course, the greater the resources entrusted to them, the greater their responsibility. Jesus picks up on this in his parable of the faithful or unfaithful slave, noting: *"From everyone to whom much has been given, much will be required; and from the one to whom much has been entrusted, even more will be demanded"* **(Luke 12:48).** Craig Blomberg puts it this way: "People in positions of power have no increased privilege—just increased responsibility!"

Acting as trustees of whatever wealth we have been given, is therefore foundational to a biblical perspective on provision and wealth. These resources are not for us to do with as we please. How we use them is not our business alone either. While God does not expect us to live on nothing, he does require us to maximize our resources for the building of God's kingdom. Those fortunate enough to be born into affluence have a responsibility to use their wealth to provide for those who don't have enough. They may accomplish this in a variety of ways, including donations, investments and direct service. The command to use our resources for the benefit of poor people is given directly in the book of Exodus: *For six years, you shall sow your land and gather in its yield; but the seventh year, you shall let it rest and lie fallow, so that the poor of your people may eat; and* what they leave, the wild animals may eat. You shall do the same with your vineyard, and with your olive orchard** (Exodus 23:10–11).

Whoever owns land has a duty to let the poor use it free of charge, one year in every seven, and even to let wild animals make use of it. This command is repeated in Deuteronomy in even simpler terms: *"Since there will never cease to be some in need on the earth, I therefore command you, 'Open your hand to the poor and needy neighbor in your land'"* **(Deuteronomy 15:11).** The crucial point is that we are not to hoard the resources entrusted to us for ourselves, maintaining lifestyles, homes and church facilities beyond what is needed.

Trusteeship reminds us who we are working for—God—and for what we are working toward—God's kingdom. It centers us in a new economy and a different dream, one framed by God's agenda for this world, and for us. As partners with God, we have been called to participate in this cause with all the resources at our disposal—including our wealth.

GRATEFULNESS
"What do you have that you did not receive?
And if you received it, why do you boast as if it were not a gift?"
1 Corinthians 4:7

If we understand that everything we have is God's—including the very capacity to work, engage in business, create and produce, sell, and build wealth—we will be grateful to God. Of course, if we are wealthy and have abundance, it's easy to convince ourselves that what we have is mainly a result of our own hard work, intelligence and creative genius. The reality is quite the opposite. If we have been born into a loving family, a prosperous country, a good educational system and a stable society with the rule of law, we have the good fortune needed to make it possible for hard work to pay off. This is not to suggest that hard work never contributes to economic success. Clearly, it is often a factor. Yet even intelligence and creative genius, needed to make hard work fruitful, are gifts from God. The apostle Paul puts it bluntly when he asks the Corinthians, **"What do you have that you did not receive? And if you received it, why do you boast as if it were not a gift?" (1 Corinthians 4:7)**

Paul's point is that even the very abilities we have are given to us by God. King David echoes this sentiment when in response to God's generosity, he prays, **"Who am I, O Lord God, and what is my house, that you have brought me thus far?" (1 Chronicles 17:16)** Biblically, the response to the blessing of provision and abundance is deep gratitude, even if our own work played a major role in generating our wealth. Yet even among Christians, affluence seems to breed ingratitude and a sense of entitlement—as if we are somehow owed something. This betrays an inflated view of our own importance, and a very limited awareness of gift, grace and good fortune in our lives.

Another factor that prevents us from experiencing gratitude is envy. It is easy to begrudge others for what they have, rather than being content and grateful for what we have, if we see ourselves primarily as consumers rather than servants. Western culture feeds this envy. Marketing, advertising and even entertainment encourage us to make living like the rich our aspiration. In doing so, we crave for what others have—not only their possessions but also their abilities and circumstances. In contrast, the Bible commands us not to covet anything that belongs to our neighbor—whether positions at work, salaries, economic opportunities or bank balances—but to develop a growing gratitude for what we have been given. How can we become more thankful? By giving thanks. We become more thankful through the simple act of giving thanks every day for whatever we have that we appreciate. Positions at work, high salaries, economic opportunities and bank balances should all compel us to give thanks and glory to the Lord.

HAPPINESS AND SATISFACTION
"Keep your lives free from the love of money
and be content with what you have."
Hebrews 13:5

Gratitude leads to contentment. Contentment is a delicious feeling, and it is the antidote to greed and envy. The Bible presents a vision for economic life that doesn't depend on ever-increasing consumption to prevent us from feeling disappointed. In this vision, it is possible to have enough and to cease longing for more. The Israelites experienced this in the wilderness, when every day God gave them exactly enough bread ("manna") from heaven. ***"Those who gathered much had nothing over, and those who gathered little had*** *no shortage; they gathered as much as each of them needed"* (Exodus 16:18). Hebrews counsels us: *"Keep your lives free from the love of money and be content with what you have"* (Hebrews 13:5).

In the same vein, Paul writes, *"Of course, there is great gain in godliness combined with contentment; for we brought nothing into the world, so that we can take nothing out of it; but if we have food and clothing, we will be content with these"* (1 Timothy 6:6–8). And in a letter written from a prison cell, Paul shares something of his own journey: *"Not that I am referring to being in need; for I have learned to be content with whatever I have. I know what it is to have little, and I know what it is to have plenty. In any and all circumstances, I have learned the secret of being well fed and of going hungry, of having plenty and of being in need. I can do all things through him who strengthens me"* (Philippians 4:11–13).

Both Paul and the far-from-wealthy Philippian church he was writing to were barely surviving economically. Their attitude of being content in all economic situations challenges those who live in plenty, to find contentment in what they have. Contentment is knowing what is enough. What is enough profit? Pay? Hours employed? Savings accumulated? House size? Possessions? Given that none of us have a true gauge on what is sufficient and what is excessive, we will need help from others. What would it be like for Christians to meet in small groups to share their purchasing plans and reflect together whether they reflect true needs leading to gratitude and contentment, or envious aspirations that will lead merely to a sense of entitlement and discontent? So few Christians have tried this, that it is hard to know what effect it might have, to simply share our ideas about what is enough in practical terms. You have the foundations of happiness if you have a roof over your head and food on the table.

GOD'S GUIDANCE

"Let the wise listen and add to their learning,
and let the discerning get guidance."
Proverbs 1:5

We can seek guidance about provision from God and expect that doing so will help us meet our needs, the needs of those who depend on us and the needs of the world. Jesus states: *"Ask, and it will be given you ... For everyone who asks receives ... Is there anyone among you who, if your child asks for bread, will give a stone? Or if the child asks for a fish, will give a snake? If you then, who are evil, know how to give good gifts to your children, how much more will your Father in heaven give good things to those who ask him!"* **(Matthew 7:7–11)** After acknowledging and thanking the church at Philippi for their gift to him while he languished in house arrest in Rome, Paul confidently states, *"My God will fully satisfy every need of yours according to his riches in glory in Christ Jesus"* **(Philippians 4:19)**.

Does this mean that if we don't have enough to provide for our needs and the needs of those around us, we should ask God for help? Yes. We do not have God's promise that he will provide everything we desire immediately. But we do have his promise to give us what we need. We should ask for his guidance in practical ways if we are in

For bonuses go to ...

need. We can ask for his guidance in finding a job, applying for benefits, changing jobs, resolving employee-employer disputes, obtaining education and job training. We should ask for his transforming power in our workplace ethics, creativity and productivity, work habits and other factors needed to keep a job and thrive in the workplace.

If we are unemployed or under-employed, our disappointment or shame may lead us to back away from God. But these are the moments to draw closer to God more than ever. Looking to God for help doesn't just apply to those who lack provision. If we have wealth, the choices in how to earn, invest and give are often bewilderingly complex. In such situations, we need God's guidance and direction in deciding how to gain and use such resources well—in ways that honor God and don't harm ourselves or others. James instructs, *"If any of you is lacking in wisdom, ask God, who gives to all generously and ungrudgingly, and it will be given to you"* **(James 1:5).** We are meant to depend on God for guidance in every conceivable aspect of our lives.

www.wisdomlaneofwealth.com

W.I.N.K.

Chapter 10

How the Godly Operate in Wealth

10

COMMITMENT TO GIVE TO GOD

*"Honor the Lord from your wealth, and from the first of a
ll your produce; so your barns will be filled with plenty,
and your vats will overflow with new wine."*
Proverbs 3:9–10

The scriptures have a lot to say on the topic of our financial commitments since we are mere stewards of the resources God has given us. Giving first to God, as quoted above, is an acknowledgement that He owns everything and that it was from Him that we are reaping the harvest. Lots of strong believers in the faith can testify how giving first to the Lord has served as a springboard for the development of their faith. As a matter of fact, giving to God can be compared to a preventative vaccination in the medical field before we get a financial pandemic.

Giving to God is a spiritual matter as well as a relational issue with Him. Giving is actually the thermometer for measuring the temperature of our spiritual health. In order to yield to God's ownership of all our possessions, we must analyze carefully what may be the most compelling evidence of our stewardship. We need to make a decision as to how much we are willing to give to God. 2

For bonuses go to ...

Corinthians 9:6–8 says: *"Each of you should give what you have decided in your heart to give, not reluctantly or under compulsion, for God loves a cheerful giver. And God is able to bless you abundantly, so that in all things at all times, having all that you need, you will abound in every good work."* Even not giving a dime to Him is a decision. As stewards, we will be held accountable for every single decision we make.

The scriptures give lots of promises to a cheerful giver. He will give us the ability to acquire wealth. **Deuteronomy 28:5** says: *"Your basket and your kneading trough will be blessed."* And in **Deuteronomy 28:12,** the Bible continues to say: *"The Lord will open the heavens, the storehouse of His bounty, to send rain on your land in season and to bless all the work of your hands. You will lend to many."* Figuratively, the Lord promises to sprinkle blessings of abundance on whatever we invest in. Moreover, He promises to protect us in a variety of ways, among which are deadly diseases, motor accidents and job security. In **Malachi 3:11,** it says: *"I will prevent pests from devouring your crops, and the vines in your fields will not drop their fruits before it is ripe."*

We really owe a financial allegiance to God the Creator for all that He does for us. He gives everything to us freely without any strings attached, and yet we keep dragging our feet when it comes to giving Him a small portion of the very resources that He Himself has given to us. He created us in His own image and likeness, so we need to imitate His character, which is manifested in His giving to all mankind. In **Romans 8:32,** the apostle Paul says something powerful about the Creator. He says: *"He who did not spare His own Son, but gave him* up for us all, how shall He not also with him freely give us all things?" Finally, God does not want quantity of gifts. Rather, He loves quality of gifts. The story of the widow's mite illustrates this point. The rich gave huge sums of money but still retained lots of their fortunes; meaning that they gave out of their abundance. But the widow's mite was her last means of financial support. In other words, she placed her sole reliance on God's provision. *"God loves a cheerful giver"* **(2 Corinthians 9:7).**

Worship always demands a gift. We cannot worship God without giving, because worship means to put worth on somebody; therefore, we bring our treasure and things we consider valuable to the King. Secondly, giving to the King attracts His favor. Whatever we give to the Lord, He will bless us because he needs to prove that He is our Creator. Lastly, by giving to the Lord, we acknowledge that He has ownership of everything we possess. Giving to the Lord is always a test to see if we are convinced that He owns everything. So, in a way, our gifts to Him are a gesture of thanksgiving.

COMMITMENT TO PAY OUR DEBTS

"The rich rule over the poor, a
nd the borrower is slave to the lender."
Proverbs 22:7

There is an adage that seems to have taken control of my whole being and it goes like this: *"If your output exceeds your income, your upkeep will be your downfall."* If each one of us would embrace this

For bonuses go to ...

piece of wisdom, debt would never wave at us. As seen from the scripture quoted above, debt enslaves us to our lenders. **Matthew 6:24** says: *"No one can serve two masters. Either you will hate the one and love the other, or you will be devoted to the one and despise the other. You cannot serve both God and money."* When we become debt-strapped and stressed about payments of our bills, money becomes an idol. This portrays debt as a real monster that can lead us into spiritual and financial bondage. Solomon, the wise man, is advising us here not to incur debts we cannot pay back. Furthermore, bad debts can also destroy our families. In the Old Testament, if you were reeling in abject poverty, you could sell your children into slavery as a relief, and till such time that the debt was entirely paid, you could never have your children back.

In **2 Kings 4:1**, we have a prime example of how monstrous debt was: *"The wife of a man from the company of the prophets cried out to Elisha, 'Your servant my husband is dead, and you know that he revered the* L<small>ORD</small>*. But now his creditor is coming to take my two boys as his slaves."* This was a terrible predicament! Unfortunately, we do not have that kind of slavery in our contemporary world, but when we become insolvent in such a way that we are unable to pay our creditors, it creates a lot of stress upon us, and this is one of the major reasons why most marriages fall apart.

The reason that the Bible is strict about debt accumulation is the fact that it drags God's name through the mud. Debt can really hurt the reputation of God. As followers of Christ, getting submerged in debt taints our reputation as well as the Holy One we are following. **Psalm 37:21** says: *"The wicked borrow and never repay, but the godly* *are generous givers."* This indicates that we are not godly as we profess to be if we do not pay our debts. Let us therefore remember that we have God's reputation at stake if we bear chains of debt around our necks. Debts really consume our lives, and repaying them honors God; it is divinely right to do that.

Debts can, however, be controlled if we manage our resources well and live within our means. First, we must admit that we have a problem, and this problem is all about greed, which is a deadly disease that engulfs our body and soul. It comes in all shapes and forms, and we need to pull up our sleeves to fight it squarely.

However, there are good debts, like mortgages, that appreciate over time. These are the only debts that are recommended. In other words, good debts have the potential to increase our net worth and give us better lives. They help us build more wealth. In contrast, bad debts are those that are used for consumption purposes or for purchasing depreciating assets. This type of debt is what we are being warned against.

COMMITMENT TO MAKE PRUDENT INVESTMENTS

"She considers a field and buys it;
from her earnings, she plants a vineyard."
Proverbs 31:16

The injunction given by God at the beginning to "be fruitful and multiply" applies to our finances as well. We need to indulge in wise

For bonuses go to ...

investments in order to multiply our money. In the verse quoted above, the godly woman is commended because she took the money she had and invested it wisely.

Jesus once told a parable in which a particular steward was scolded for failing to multiply the money given to him by not investing it. This parable is set in the context of investments. A rich man delegates the management of his wealth to his servants. He gives five talents to the first servant, two talents to the second and one talent to the third. Two of the servants earn 100% returns by investing the funds they received, but the third servant hides the money under the ground and earns nothing in return. The rich man returns from his journey, rewards the two servants who made profits, but punishes harshly the servant who made no profit. The rich man said: **"You wicked, lazy servant! So you knew that I harvest where I have not sown and gather where I have not scattered seed? Well then, you should have put my money on deposit with the bankers, so that when I returned, I would have received it back with interest" (Matthew 25:14–30).** This parable is strong evidence that the scriptures endorse wise investments. Investing can be compared to the act of planting seeds. What we invest wisely is not gone and wasted; rather, it is growing.

www.wisdomlaneofwealth.com

PROVISION FOR THE POOR AMONG US

"There is one who scatters, yet increases all the more, and there is one who withholds what is justly due, but it results only in want. The generous man will be prosperous, and he who waters will himself be watered. He who withholds grain, the people will curse him, but blessing will be on the head of him who sells it."
Proverbs 11:24–26

As Christians, we are blessed to be a blessing to the poor and the needy. This is all the more reason that God's plan is to make us prosperous. **Jeremiah 29:11 says:** *"For I know the plans I have for you, declares the Lord, plans to prosper you and not to harm you, plans to give you hope and a future."* Neglecting the poor and the needy, such as widows and orphans, is a wicked gesture in the sight of the Lord. **Proverbs 14:21 says:** *"He who despises his neighbor sins, but happy is he who is gracious to the poor."* The good news is: *"He who is gracious to a poor man lends to the Lord, and He will repay him for his good deed"* **(Proverbs 19:17).** This is an amazing revelation that should spur us on to help the needy.

The Book of Proverbs is replete with verses that emphasize attention to the poor. In **Proverbs 28:27**, it says: *"He who gives to the poor will never want, but he who shuts his eyes will have many curses."* Sometimes we try to probe deeply into the conditions of a needy person before digging into our pockets to help them out. Jesus did not do that. For instance, when feeding thousands of people with a loaf of bread and five pieces of fish, He did not probe into why they left home without bringing enough food with them. The moment He realized that they were hungry, He just fed them. That is exactly what we have to do when we are helping others. Let us look at what a wife of a noble character does to the poor: *"She opens her arms to the poor and extends her hands to the needy"* (Proverbs 31:20).

There is another interesting area that the Lord wants us to use our wealth for. It is found in **Proverbs 31:8–9:** *"Speak up for those who cannot speak for themselves, for the rights of all who are destitute. Speak up and judge fairly; defend the rights of the poor and needy."* Here, the scriptures are giving us instructions on some of the roles for which the wealth we have acquired should be used to play in the lives of the poor. Most poor people easily fall prey to injustice in our judiciary system due to poverty. The Lord is drawing the attention of the wealthy to look into such areas and invest in the victory of the poor concerning injustice. Finally, *"It is more blessed to give than to receive"* (Acts 20:35).

PROVISION OF INHERITANCE FOR POSTERITY

"A good man leaves an inheritance to his children's children, and the wealth of the sinner is stored up for the righteous."
Proverbs 13:22

This verse highlights one extra quality of a good and wealthy person; it shows that he thinks generationally. He simply does not make provision for his children's future but for his grandchildren's as well. Biblically, an inheritance does not refer to the passing on of real estate and other possessions from one generation to another, but it also refers to the earthly and spiritual gifts that God plans to give to those who are His children. In this particular instance, the divine book is instructing us on one vital area on which we need to spend our wealth. We do not have to consume our riches on ourselves. Clothes, shoes and furniture are not inheritance. An inheritance that consists of durable and appreciative assets like real estate is what is being spoken about here. We need to leave them something that will help them get a home to live in or a solid financial means to help them live comfortable lives.

A good man handles money and goods wisely in accordance with divine principles like prudence and kindness. **Proverbs 11:25** says: *"A generous person will prosper; whoever refreshes others will be refreshed."* Furthermore, a good man does not spend in accordance with the desires of the flesh or the pride of life; he spends his resources as a trustworthy steward of what the Lord has entrusted to him. He is also happy with whatever he has and, therefore, does not feel compelled to spend more than he should. He deems everything he possesses as the Lord's and not his own. He prudently lives within his means, invests the surplus of his money and buys appreciative assets to leave to his children and grandchildren as an inheritance.

Best of all, a good man recognizes that the most important legacy is not just material wealth, but a Christ-like character and a good name. Passing on spiritual inheritance is a legacy that can never be lost. When we leave them with knowledge of the scriptures and divine wisdom, they will be wealthy for eternity.

For bonuses go to ...

As stated in the scriptures quoted above, the wicked man is bound to leave his inheritance to the righteous because, though he lives a wealthy life for a while, he will eventually die and bequeath his wealth to others. Since he acquired his wealth in an ungodly way, he might have led a wicked life, which his children might have copied; and they would most likely waste his wealth and ultimately pass it on to wise family members who are godly.

www.wisdomlaneofwealth.com

W.I.N.K.

Chapter 11

Types of Wealth

SPIRITUAL WEALTH

"For what shall it profit a man,
if he shall gain the whole world and lose his own soul?
Or what shall a man give in exchange for his soul?"
Mark 8:36

Each time we talk about wealth, we normally cast our minds on money. I personally do not share this view. Wealth is a state of mind and there are a couple of areas we need to be wealthy in before we can claim that accolade. The first and foremost area of wealth we should all aspire to acquire is the spiritual realm. If our spiritual wealth is in disarray and we have billions of dollars at the bank, we are the poorest entity on Earth. The scripture quoted above is a strong indicator of our wretchedness if we lack a divine contact with our Creator. It entails being rich toward God.

In **Luke 12:34**, Jesus says: *"Where your treasure is, there will your heart be also,"* indicating that the location of our money demonstrates the location of our hearts. Now, one thing we have to bear in mind is that money is a two-edged sword. Wherever we spend our money is where our hearts lie. We exchange our wealth for what we value or treasure. It could be in the entertainment industry or church ministries for the propagation of God's word. Therefore, if I say that money is a two-edged sword, it means that it has the capacity to reveal that you value certain things more than the Creator (which is risky), or that you value the Creator more than earthly things (which is godly). The money itself is valueless, but how it is used betrays the treasures of your heart.

John 17:3 says: *"This is eternal life that they know you the only true God, and Jesus Christ whom you have sent."* Life actually does not consist of money and things; it is to know God. So we need to be spiritually wealthy. In the parable of the rich fool, the rich man produced abundantly and thought to himself, *"What shall I do, for I have nowhere to store my crops? And he said, I will do this: I will tear down my barns and build larger ones, and there I will store all my grain and my goods. And I will say to my soul, 'Soul, you have ample goods laid up for many years; relax, eat, drink, be merry.' But God said to him, 'Fool! This night your soul will be required of you, and the things you have prepared, whose will they be?'"* This is what I mean by the one who lays up treasure for himself but is not wealthy toward God.

The fact is, it is not evil when our "land produces plentifully," as in **verse 16.** There is nothing sinister about our business prospering and more money flowing into our coffers. It is not evil when our investments soar in value. That is not the evil in this parable. He is not branded a fool for being an industrious farmer. Rather, he is called a fool by the way he used the increase of his wealth. There was no indication of being wealthy toward God. It was good to build larger barns if he were storing the grain for a use that shows God is our treasure. It is what the farmer says to his soul: *"Soul, you have ample goods laid up for many years; relax, eat, drink, be merry."* It is the use he plans to make of his wealth, which does indicate that he treasures his riches more than God; that is where his foolishness stems from. We must, therefore, be spiritually wealthy toward God.

INTELLECTUAL WEALTH

"For the protection of wisdom is like the protection of money, and the advantage of knowledge is that wisdom preserves the life of him who has it."
Ecclesiastes 7:12

The second area of wealth we need to engage ourselves in is the intellectual and emotional realm. We must concentrate on developing ourselves intellectually. The Creator gave us a massive empty brain that needs to be developed to the fullest. This can only happen when we enrich our souls with knowledge. Our soul comprises of our mind, our will, and our emotions. The importance of acquiring knowledge cannot be overemphasized. The adage has it that a fool and his money are soon parted. It is not beneficial to have billions of dollars in our bank accounts but lack the cleverness to invest it appropriately to yield more.

Solomon was a champion in this sphere of wealth. At his enthronement as King of Israel, he requested nothing but wisdom from the Lord, and the Creator was happy with it and responded by

For bonuses go to ...

saying: *"I will do what you have asked. I will give you a wise and discerning heart, so that there will never have been anyone like you, nor will there ever be. ¹³ Moreover, I will give you what you have not asked for—both wealth and honor—so that in your lifetime you will have no equal among kings"* **(1 Kings 3:12–13)**. Here we see the Lord blessing him with immense riches because he asked for wisdom.

Later, during his kinship, he had this to say: *"**Blessed are those who find wisdom, those who gain understanding, for she is more profitable than silver, and yields better returns than gold"* **(Proverbs 3:13–14)**. Solomon is confessing here that wisdom gives birth to wealth. I am compelled to believe that our prosperity depends on our intellectual development. When we cast a quick glance at most of the billionaires in our contemporary world, we see that they are mostly people who had ideas to create stuff that brings solutions to human problems. A typical example is Steve Jobs with his invention of the iPhone and the iPad. All communication gaps in ancient times have been bridged with his ideas.

The importance of intellectual wealth is also pointed out in **3 John 1:2: *"Beloved, I pray that you may prosper in all things and be in health, just as your soul prospers."*** This is a striking illustration that our health depends, to a large extent, on our mental state.

www.wisdomlaneofwealth.com

PHYSICAL AND MENTAL WEALTH

"Beloved, I pray that all may go well with you and that you may be in good health, as it goes well with your soul."
3 Peter 1:2

Another area of wealth that commands our attention is that of health. In the biblical verse quoted above, we are strongly encouraged to remain physically fit. The adage says that "health is wealth," and we can all testify to this fact. It renders a decisive meaning to our life since health is viewed as the most precious asset every human being needs to possess. Good health does not solely comprise of the absence of diseases in our body but complete physical, mental, social and spiritual wellness. Steve Jobs was worth billions of dollars, but at the point of death, not a dime could save his life from pancreatic cancer. He passed away, leaving billions of dollars in his bank accounts. Sadly enough, he was endowed with material wealth, but he could not enjoy it because he lacked physical wealth. **Proverbs 11:4 says:** *"Wealth is worthless in the day of wrath, but righteousness delivers from death."* Money cannot protect us from death. We might cheat the righteous and trust in our wealth on this Earth. But one day, we will leave this Earth, and our money cannot extend our life past the point where God has ordained that it will end. The Bible says in **Psalm 49:12:** *"People, despite their wealth, do not endure; they are like the beasts that perish."* This is real food for thought!

It does not matter how wealthy you are in terms of talents, ideas and divine gifts. If your health is not in good shape, you are still classified as poor and wretched. This is a warning to us all to strive for physical wealth instead of material wealth. No wonder God issued laws pertaining to hygiene and physical health to the Israelites. He prescribed specific food regarding what to eat and what to steer away from. This indicates that God is very particular about our health. We need to embark on regular exercise, avoid alcohol and drugs, as well as eat a balanced diet to remain healthy.

This tells us that some of the most important things that are better than wealth are good health and eternal life (time). On our deathbeds, what we would crave for is the restoration of our health and more time to live instead of more money to spend. Health is wealth, says the wise man. Mental health includes our emotional, psychological and social well-being. Good mental health affects how we think, feel and act. It is vital at every stage of our lives, and we need to cherish it more than wealth.

SOCIAL WEALTH

"Walk with the wise and become wise,
for a companion of fools suffers harm."
Proverbs 13:20

One area of wealth that normally escapes our attention is our social wealth. But the importance of this sphere cannot be overemphasized. We need to be wealthy in our family, friendship and social relationships. As a matter of fact, we are as poor as the friends we have. The flip side also applies. We are as wealthy as the friends we keep in our lives. The adage that best describes this situation is, "Birds of the same feather flock together." The wise King Solomon says, in **Proverbs 27:17:** *"As iron sharpens iron, so one person sharpens another."* Who do we associate ourselves with? We need to choose our associations wisely.

Building healthy relationships is one of the most important components of our health and well-being. Evidence based on research indicates that strong relationships contribute to a long, healthy and happy life. Inversely, being alone or isolating ourselves in life poses a couple of health risks such as obesity and high blood pressure. Our marital relationships need to be enriched as well; otherwise, all our riches are worthless. If the relationships with our parents and siblings leave much to be desired, then we are socially poor. This is why Jesus stressed the importance of forgiving one another. In **Luke 6:27–28,** He advises us: *"But to you who are listening, I say: Love your enemies, do good to those who hate you, bless those who curse you, pray for those who mistreat you."* This is a powerful message for our social wealth! He is advising us to do good to everyone because we never know whom our prosperity in life may depend on. We are to pray for even those who persecute us, because our wealth may come from them.

Sometimes we do not need money to make money. Rather, we need influential people to connect us to jobs, businesses, sponsorships and scholarships. The poor company we keep makes us poorer all the time. Joseph's experience in Egypt highlights the importance of building our social wealth. Let us watch the strategies he used to get out of prison and become a prime minister. He made up his mind to

For bonuses go to ...

develop strong relationships with his inmates. He struck up an acquaintance with two people who knew Pharaoh well, and even interpreted their dreams for them. And he pleaded with them that if they were released from prison, they should remember him. When one of them was released and managed to get his job back in Pharaoh's office, he recommended Joseph to Pharaoh when the King had a dream he couldn't remember and none of his sages could interpret it. The friend who was a wine servant told Pharaoh that he knew a young Jewish man who could interpret his dream. "I know," in social wealth vocabulary, means to have "connections and relationships" with influential people. Most of us have the wrong people in our social circles, and that is why we never get promotions in our workplaces. In short, it was "connections and relationships" that cleared the path for a prisoner like Joseph to become the prime minister of Egypt. We have to be wealthy in our social relationships.

www.wisdomlaneofwealth.com

W.I.N.K.

Chapter 12

Things That Are Better Than Wealth

12

INTEGRITY

*"A good name is more desirable than great riches;
to be esteemed is better than silver or gold."*
Proverbs 22:1

No matter whom we are, people always carry a suitcase of information about us. When our names crop up in their minds, all they think of is our reputation. The information they have about us is based on nothing but our actions, attitudes, appearance and the sort of words that come out of our mouths each time we speak. The data people hold about us stems from whether we are moral or immoral, kind or wicked, patient or prone to anger, selfish or generous. In a vast majority of cases, the information they harbor about us is based on what other people say about us. **Proverbs 20:11** says: *"Even a child is known by his doings, whether his work be pure, and whether it be right."*

A mere silly misbehavior can drag our reputation through the mud. At times, this misdemeanor can be redressed, but sometimes it taints our character for the rest of our lives. Those who care less about their fame, throw caution to the wind and behave in any way they want. **Matthew 5:16** cautions us: *"Let your light so shine before men, that they may see your good works, and glorify your father which is in heaven."* We are, therefore, compelled to lead exemplary lives so that we can retain a classic reputation that is worthy of emulation and is a strong testimony for Christ.

Our integrity needs to be protected all the time. **Proverbs 19:1** says: *"Better is the poor man who walks in his integrity than one who is perverse in his lips and is a fool."* In this verse, Solomon is making a contrast between a poor man and a fool. Seemingly, this poverty-stricken man is someone who fears God and seeks His wisdom. There is nothing condemnatory about being poor if we fear God and live wisely. In contrast, the fool is someone who invests his trust, confidence and salvation in something foolish rather than in God. Lots of poor people are fools, but since this fool is being contrasted with a poor man, he is more likely to be a wealthy man. Being wealthy is not evil, but putting all our trust in our riches makes us fools. **1 Timothy 6:17** says: *"Charge them that are rich in this world, that they be not high-minded, nor trust in uncertain riches, but in the living God, who giveth us richly all things to enjoy."* The rich man is *perverse in his ways*. The word "perverse" here means corrupt, and that means his ways are twisted. He follows a twisted and perverted path in life, which is parallel to God's way. It twists and bends through all the crooked ways of achieving wealth. Being extraordinary rich, he leads a life that is full of vanity, just as the prodigal son.

The principles we need to glean from the above instances are many. First, we need to understand that wealth cannot be compared with integrity. It is not as relevant as a good reputation. The scriptures make it clear that integrity is the key to godliness but not wealth. Secondly, whether we are rich or living in abject poverty, God is only interested in our character. He judges us by what goes on in our hearts. As a result, we need to walk constantly in uprightness, making sure our integrity is untainted. **Proverbs 28:6** says: *"Better is a poor man who walks in his integrity than a rich man who is crooked in his ways."*

A PEACEFUL HOME THAT IS FILLED WITH LOVE

"Better is a dry morsel and quietness with it,
than a house full of feasting with strife."
Proverbs 17:1

A countless number of homes are led to the altar of sacrifice in a bid to earn money, most often under the guise of providing for the family. The scripture quoted above admonishes us to strive for a home that is full of love and harmony, rather than one that possesses money. **Proverbs 15:17** says: *"Better a small serving of vegetables with love than a fattened calf with hatred."* In other words, it is better to have a scanty supply and still fear God than to have a surplus of wealth and trouble. It is better to have love in the family and eat a simple meal of vegetables than to eat a gorgeous meal with meats while there is strife in the family.

The Lord's presence is felt in a home where peace reigns. In **Luke 10:5–7,** Jesus instructs His disciples to look for a home where there is peace, whilst they go out to preach. He also instructed them to stay only in such homes and never search for others. Our homes are supposed to be the sanctuaries for God. If all husbands and wives could grasp this principle, our homes would be heaven on Earth. Unity is the key to running a peaceful home. When couples have a heart of forgiveness and are ready to forgive themselves, harmony will forever become part and parcel of their lives. We should endeavor to alleviate anger by following the advice Solomon gives us in **Proverbs 15:18:** *"A gentle answer turns away wrath, but a harsh word stirs up anger. The tongue of the wise adorns knowledge, but the mouth of the fool gushes folly."* This is one of the wonderful verses for families to learn together. If we all demonstrate kindness to each other, peace will flow like a river in our homes.

Peace is something more than the absence of strife in the family; it is the existence of happiness. There are three types of peace we need to possess: peace with God, peace within our hearts and peace within our relationships with others. **Romans 14:19** says: *"Let us, therefore, follow after the things which make for peace, and things with which one may edify another."* In short, peace should be nurtured in our hearts before it can permeate the hearts of those we live with. It is the barometer for measuring our spiritual pressure; and therefore, the absence of peace is a warning of low spirituality within us. **Matthew 5:9** says: *"Blessed are the peacemakers, for they shall be called sons of God."*

WISDOM

"Do not forsake wisdom, and she will protect you; love her, and she will watch over you. Wisdom is supreme; therefore, get wisdom. Though it cost all you have, get understanding."
Proverbs 4:6–7

The scriptures prescribe two paths to take in life: wisdom and foolishness. Both paths are like parallel lines and, no matter how far they are extended, they never meet. Furthermore, these two paths produce different outcomes. The Bible is replete with admonition to choose the path of wisdom. It is the only way that leads us to spiritual and material prosperity. The verses quoted above, urge us to do everything we can to acquire wisdom at all costs. The only way we become wise is by giving reverence to God. Wisdom helps us in a variety of ways, and we all have access to it by reading the scriptures and asking Him. **James 1:5** says: *"If any of you lacks wisdom, you should ask God, who gives generously to all without finding fault, and it will be given to you."*

Wisdom is the application of God's laws and principles. That is why the scriptures admonish us to acquire it at all costs. We need to be wise in order to be successful and wealthy in life. Sometimes we memorize God's laws to such an extent that we know them to the letter. But the problem lies in the fact that we do not apply them in our practical life, and that is what the Bible calls foolishness. Till such time that we walk the talk, we will never gain wisdom. When we know these laws and principles and yet put their application out of the equation, we fail in whatever we do. However, the application is what

For bonuses go to ...

pleases God, and that is what makes us wealthy. The secret of Joshua's success was his reliance on God and the obedience of His commandments. **Joshua 1:8** says: *"Do not let this book of the law depart from your mouth, but meditate on it day and night, that you may be careful to do everything that is written in it. Then you will be prosperous and successful."*

Solomon's crush on wisdom stems from the superiority of it over silver and gold. His choice of wisdom over everything else should send home a strong message to us. It indicates that wisdom attracts wealth and prosperity. God's reaction to his request is amazing: *" ... see, I have given you a wise and understanding heart ... and I have also given you what you have not asked: both riches and honor, so that there shall not be anyone like you among the kings all of your days"* **(1 Kings 3:11–13)**. These verses indicate that when we ask God for stuff we feel we need, we actually set limits on the most important blessings He has in store for us. So instead of pursuing wealth, we should rather seek to acquire wisdom. **Proverbs 8:11** says: *"... wisdom is better than rubies, and all the things one may desire cannot be compared with her."* In all our business dealings, marital relationships and community lives, wisdom is a requisite for success. In **Job 28:12–23**, Job asked what all of us need to ask: *"But where can wisdom be found? God understands its way, and He knows its place."* When we pray for divine wisdom instead of worldly material things, God is ever ready to shower on us things we never dreamt about.

www.wisdomlaneofwealth.com

TIME

*"Teach us to number our days,
that we may gain a heart of wisdom."*
Psalm 90:12

We can always find a means of making more money, but we can never add an extra hour to the day. We cannot give ourselves 10 extra years on Earth by investing in the "time market." Every human being at the verge of death has just one wish. We all wish we could be granted more years to live but not more money to spend. This makes time more important than money. The scriptures, therefore, advise us to make a wise use of our time because time wasted can never be regained. On the other hand, wasted money can be regained somehow.

Time is the currency of our lives, not money. Time is the currency we need to invest in, in order to fulfill our dreams and to accomplish all that God has given us. It is also the measure of life. We are all products of how we use our time. Whatever we have in life is what we used our time to purchase. Every decision we make at the present is going to shape our future lives.

For bonuses go to ...

FAITH IN GOD AND EVERLASTING LIFE

"Cast but a glance at riches, and they are gone, for they will surely sprout wings and fly off to the sky like an eagle."
Proverbs 23:5

This verse summarizes the lens through which wealth should be viewed. It tells us that riches are ephemeral and cannot be relied upon for eternal joy. The only thing on Earth that is worth pursuing is reliance on the Almighty God and His words. A fantasy story is told of a real estate mogul who was visited by an angel one night, who offered to supply any need he requested. The mogul asked for a magazine on real estate market prices in the next two years. As he was glancing through the magazine at the incredible high prices of houses in his area, and musing on how much money he would make out of his investments, he saw his picture in an obituary column. All of a sudden, his smile of prosperity turned into tears of sorrow and desperation in view of his impending death.

The scriptures tell us, in **Ecclesiastes 5:15**: *"Everyone comes naked from their mother's womb, and as everyone comes, so they depart. They take nothing from their toil that they can carry in their hands."* This is a striking illustration of the futility of wealth that is acquired and used ungodly. God wants us to trust Him with a childlike faith, which may not know what is ahead but that holds tight to the hand of a loving Father. **Matthew 16:26** says: *"For what will it profit a man if he gains the whole world and forfeits his soul? Or what shall a man give in return for his soul?"* Let us not gain the world and lose our souls. Eternal life is all that matters. **John 3:16** says: *"For God so loved*

www.wisdomlaneofwealth.com

the world that he gave his only begotten Son, that whoever believes in Him shall not perish but have eternal life." This is the best thing we should strive for in life—not ungodly riches.

We are exhorted in **Matthew 6:19–21** as follows: ***"Do not store up for yourselves treasures on earth, where moths and vermin destroy, and where thieves break in and steal, but lay up for yourselves treasures in heaven, where neither moth nor rust destroys and where thieves do not break in and steal. For where your treasure is, there your heart will be also."*** Treasures that are temporary are subject to deterioration and destruction, just as Jesus illustrates in His examples of moths and rust. They will eventually expire in one way or the other. Treasures such as faith, hope and love echo sentiments Paul shares in his letter to the Corinthian Church, in **1 Corinthians 13:13**. Integrity, character and sound speech are highly encouraged in his letter to Titus in **Titus 2:7**. When we use the gifts, talents and wealth God has given us, to impact the world for His kingdom work, we lay up treasures in heaven. Having faith in the Almighty God—that He created us and owns everything in the universe, and that He gave His only beloved Son for us to believe in and have eternal life—is better than material wealth that is ungodly dispensed.

For bonuses go to www.wisdomlaneofwealth.com

W.I.N.K.

Chapter 13

The Synopsis: Is God Against Wealth and Prosperity?

*S*tep into the Wisdom Lane of Wealth has demonstrated that the zeal to be wealthy is neither sinful nor satanic. It proves beyond reasonable doubt that wealth is never of the devil. In **Haggai 2:8**, we read this: *"The silver is mine, and the gold is mine, says the Lord of Hosts."* This is an amazing verse that supports the claim that wealth originates from God. So, the question that lends itself for asking is, why entertain the thought that we cannot be rich or wealthy as believers?" The Lord is the custodian of wealth and prosperity. Therefore, we need to erase the mindset that wealth is sinful and devilish and is meant for a category of people. Wealth is a marvelous tool if, and only if, we use it as stewards for the Lord. The dangers of it lie in the adoption of a worldly perspective toward it.

Poverty and its attendant lack and wants should not be entertained in our lives. Efforts to live an average life should be viewed as mediocrity. God wants us to flourish in wealth because other people's lives and destinies hang on our blessings. If we decide to settle for mediocrity and marginalized lives, the needy in our communities and family circles will suffer. Poverty is not God's will for us. This is what the Lord says in **Jeremiah 29:11:** *"For I know the plans I have for you, declares the LORD, plans to prosper you and not harm you; plans to give you hope and a future."*

For bonuses go to ...

Our prosperity is essential to God because His reputation will be tarnished if we fail in life. We are products of His manufacturing company, and that is why He put His seal on us in the form of His image, right from creation. Just as manufacturing companies give manuals to ensure proper functioning of their products, so has God given us the Bible, with commandments to follow that will generate wealth for our well-being. Obedience to these laws and precepts will guarantee prosperity for us. Laws are designed to protect us and not to harm us, so we need to take great delight in the commandments of the Lord. He commands us to: *"Be fruitful and multiply; and fill the earth and subdue it and have dominion over the fish of the sea and over the birds of the heavens, and over every living thing that moves on the earth"* **(Genesis 1:26–28).** These verses indicate that human beings are superior to all other creatures that God made. The Bible says: *"... in the image of God He created them; male and female, He created them."* If we were created in His image, then it means we have the potential to create as well.

God favors divine means of acquiring wealth and using it for His kingdom work. This is all the more reason He goes to the extent of putting forth key precepts we can follow to attain righteous wealth and prosperity. First and foremost, He commands us to become of ourselves by exploring and developing our innate talents and gifts that He has planted in each one of us, as explained earlier on. The scriptures give us blueprints and strategies to achieve wealth immensely. **Genesis 1:28** encodes the secret to prosperity: *"And God blessed them, and God said to them, Be fruitful and multiply, and replenish the earth and subdue it and have dominion over the fish of the sea and over the birds of the air, and over every living thing* *that moves upon the earth."* Apart from the injunction to procreate and populate the earth, this verse is pregnant with business ideas that are meant to bestow wealth and prosperity on mankind. The blueprint revealed here is to build a business as a means of entering the wisdom lane of wealth.

A business is any problem-solving venture in which people are more than willing to pay you a substantial amount of money when you can solve their problems. It could be an enterprise providing products and services. God created us with gifts and talents, and it is our duty to discover them and engage in businesses relative to them. If we are to subdue and have dominion over the kind of business we do, we need to ensure that it creates value. Our businesses will become valuable when we do it with excellence and strive to be at our best all the time. Our wealth is in our business in most cases.

Furthermore, engaging in multiple streams of income is also a divine injunction. **Ecclesiastes 11:6** says: *"Sow your seed in the morning, and at evening let your hands not be idle, for you do not know which will succeed, whether this or that, or whether both will do equally well…."* This verse reinforces the fact that wealth increases when we have multiple vessels through which cash flows in our direction.

He also prescribes numerous other principles we should adhere to in order to swim in the currents of prosperity. One of these precepts is diligence. In **Deuteronomy 28:1–2**, it says: *"Now it shall come to pass, if you diligently obey the voice of the LORD your God, to observe carefully all His commandments which I command you* today, that the LORD your God will set you high above all nations of the earth. And all these blessings shall come upon you and overtake you, because you obey the voice of the LORD your God."* Here we see God's enthusiasm in His children's prosperity. **Psalm 1:1–3** even adds more beauty to the idea of God's affinity for divine wealth: *"Blessed is the man that walketh not in the counsel of the ungodly; nor standeth in the way of sinners, nor sitteth in the seat of the scornful. But his delight is in the law of the Lord, and in his law doth he meditate day and night. And he shall be like a tree planted by the rivers of water, that bringeth forth his fruit in his season; his leaf also shall not wither; and whatsoever he doeth shall prosper."* These verses and several others mentioned earlier on are proof of the fact that God is not against wealth and prosperity.

The Creator's work on planet Earth needs our wealth to propel it. God wants us to be wealthy so that we can contribute enormously toward the expansion of His kingdom. When we are selfless enough to use the wealth we acquire for His work on Earth, we are invariably establishing His will on Earth as it is in the celestial courts. We should therefore aspire to be wealthy. We really have to dream big by not accepting only to be rich but to be wealthy. Nelson Mandela once said: *"There is no passion to be found in playing small—in settling for a life that is less than the one you are capable of living."* This resonates very well with the divine injunction to be wealthy. True prosperity is the ability to use God's power to meet the needs of mankind in all spheres of life. And the Lord is teaching and training us how to use that wealth. The scriptures teach us how to become experts at managing God's finances.

In **1 Timothy 6:17–18,** we are taught how to operate in godly wealth. We are not to be high-minded or arrogant; neither should we trust in the uncertainty of riches but should vest all our trust in the everlasting God, who is the source of everything we possess. God needs workers for His kingdom work, and it takes money to do that these days. Feeding the poor, widows and orphans in all parts of the undeveloped countries requires a big chunk of money. Most importantly, building churches across the globe and spreading the gospel to unbelievers is a financial burden that takes money to accomplish. This is why the Almighty God is interested in blessing us with wealth. Riches are only good if they are acquired in a godly manner and used in divine ways for His kingdom work. Throughout the scriptures, there is a strong connection between God and money, with many valuable lessons we can use in our personal lives.

Deuteronomy 8:18 says: *"But remember the LORD your God, for it is He who gives you the ability to produce wealth, and so confirms His covenant, which he swore to your ancestors, as it is today."* This is a striking illustration that money and wealth are only possible through God, since it is He who is the source of all our provisions. It is He who gives the ability to make money. So, if all wealth comes from Him, then He can never be against prosperity that does not leave Him out of the equation. The Bible touches on the importance of giving to others. A classic example comes from **2 Corinthians 9:7,** which says: *"Each man should give what he has decided in his heart to give, not reluctantly or under compulsion, for God loves a cheerful giver."* Finally, God instructs us to use His gifts and blessings for good causes, and to help the needy with the wealth He has given us.

Nevertheless, the Bible repeatedly sounds caution to ill-gotten wealth and its ungodly usage. In **1 Timothy 6:10**, it reminds us: ***"For the love of money is the root of all kinds of evil. It is through this craving that some have wandered away from the faith and pierced themselves with many pangs."*** Then, in **Proverbs 23:4–5**, it says: ***"Do not wear yourself out to get rich; do not trust your own cleverness. Cast but a glance at riches and they are gone, for they will surely sprout wings and fly off the sky like an eagle."*** The scriptures also warn us against being greedy and putting money before everything else, including God. **Hebrews 13:5** instructs us: ***"Keep your life free from love of money, and be content with what you have, for He has said, I will never leave you nor forsake you."*** The scriptures further remind us, in **Matthew 6:24,** of who we truly serve: ***"No one can serve two masters, for either he will hate the one and love the other, or he will be devoted to the one and despise the other. You cannot serve God and money."*** These verses tell us that we should be glad about the gifts God has blessed us with and not to be greedy. They also speak about the fact that God is more important than money, and that we should focus on serving Him more than multiplying our wealth excessively.

DIVINE STEPS TO PROSPERITY

- The journey to the land of prosperity begins with the discovery of our purpose in life. It is an indispensable tool for achieving success. Nothing compares to honoring our divine calling, because it is the reason we were born. Discovering and developing our purpose is the work of life, and the meaning of life is serving society with our gifts. If we are struggling to figure out what our purpose in life is, then we need to fish out our passion. Our passion will definitely lead us to the shores of our purpose. Discovering what to live for gives concrete meaning to life. Life without purpose is the worst tragedy that can ever befall mankind.

- To be capable of seeing our purpose in pictures, we need to develop a sense of perception, since we cannot go the way that is invisible to us. We must not permit other people's restricted perceptions to define us, since their perceptions may not be our reality.

- We need to have a deep comprehension of our potential. Believing in our potential more than other people's assessment of us is essential to entering the wisdom lane of wealth. Our potential lies in our untapped abilities.

- Having a strong passion is an essential key to prosperity. Passion is the energy that fuels what excites us. It is a feeling that reveals to us the right thing to do in life. Chasing our passion will definitely lead us to our purpose.

- Have principles in life. We may have purpose, visions and passions in life, but only principles and obedience to divine laws can protect them. The reason principles and obedience to divine laws is so vital is because principles make life predictable.

- To become wealthy and prosperous, we need to apply the "law of planning." Having a goal without a plan or a strategy to achieve it is a mere wish.

- Associate with high achievers. This is the "law of people." If you are going to be wealthy, you need to gather in your life the right people and avoid the wrong people who are merely dream killers.

- You are bound to face resistance since there are people who will not believe you. You can use the "law of persistence."

- Use the "law of perseverance." You will need to fight to accomplish your vision. In other words, you will need to get up each time you fall.

- Use the most powerful divine tool: the "law of prayer." Pray constantly and stay connected to the source of your purpose for spiritual power.

BIBLICAL QUOTES ON WEALTH AND MONEY

The blessing of the Lord brings wealth, without painful toil for it. **Proverbs 10:22**

Do not toil to acquire wealth; be discerning enough to desist. When your eyes light on it, it is gone, for suddenly it sprouts wings, flying like an eagle toward heaven. **Proverbs 23:4–5**

Those who want to get rich fall into temptation and a trap, and into many foolish and harmful desires that plunge people into ruin and destruction. **1 Timothy 6:9**

Whoever loves money never has enough; whoever loves wealth is never satisfied with their income. This too is meaningless. **Ecclesiastes 5:10**

Honor the Lord with your wealth, with the first fruits of all your crops. **Proverbs 3:9**

Better a little with the fear of the Lord than great wealth with turmoil. **Proverbs 15:16**

For bonuses go to ...

Then he said to them, "Watch out! Be on your guard against all kinds of greed; life does not consist in an abundance of possessions." **Luke 12:15**

For where your treasure is, there your heart will be also. **Matthew 6:21**

Give to everyone what you owe them: If you owe taxes, pay taxes; if revenue, then revenue; if respect, then respect; if honor, then honor. **Romans 13:7**

How much better to get wisdom than gold, to get insight rather than silver! **Proverbs 16:16**

But who am I, and who are my people, that we should be able to give as generously as this? Everything comes from you, and we have given you only what comes from your hand. **1 Chronicles 29:14**

Command those who are rich in this present world not to be arrogant nor to put their hope in wealth, which is so uncertain, but to put their hope in God, who richly provides us with everything for our enjoyment. **1 Timothy 6:17**

Keep falsehood and lies far from me; give me neither poverty nor riches, but give me only my daily bread. **Proverbs 30:8**

What a person desires is unfailing love; better to be poor than a liar. **Proverbs 19:22**

Better the little that the righteous have than the wealth of many wicked; for the power of the wicked will be broken, but the Lord upholds the righteous. **Psalm 37:16–17**

For the love of money is the root of all kinds of evil. Some people, eager for money, have wandered from the faith and pierced themselves with many griefs. **1 Timothy 6:10**

Cast but a glance at riches, and they are gone, for they will surely sprout wings and fly off to the sky like an eagle. **Proverbs 23:5**

A good name is more desirable than great riches; to be esteemed is better than silver or gold. **Proverbs 22:1**

This is also why you pay taxes, for the authorities are God's servants, who give their full time to governing. **Romans 13:6**

Ill-gotten treasures have no lasting value, but righteousness delivers from death. **Proverbs 10:2**

Wealth is worthless in the day of wrath, but righteousness delivers from death. **Proverbs 11:4**

I rejoice in following your statutes as one rejoices in great riches. **Psalm 119:14**

For the Lord your God will bless you as he has promised, and you will lend to many nations but will borrow from none. You will rule over many nations but none will rule over you. **Deuteronomy 15:6**

For bonuses go to ...

Suppose one of you wants to build a tower. Won't you first sit down and estimate the cost to see if you have enough money to complete it? **Luke 14:28**

I know what it is to be in need, and I know what it is to have plenty. I have learned the secret of being content in any and every situation, whether well fed or hungry, whether living in plenty or in want. **Philippians 4:12**

Moreover, when God gives someone wealth and possessions, and the ability to enjoy them, to accept their lot and be happy in their toil, this is a gift of God. **Ecclesiastes 5:19**

No one can serve two masters. Either you will hate the one and love the other, or you will be devoted to the one and despise the other. You cannot serve both God and money. **Matthew 6:24**

If anyone has material possessions and sees a brother or sister in need but has no pity on them, how can the love of God be in that person? **1 John 3:17**

Wealth and honor come from you; you are the ruler of all things. In your hands are strength and power to exalt and give strength to all. **1 Chronicles 29:12**

The Lord sends poverty and wealth; he humbles and he exalts. **1 Samuel 2:7**

www.wisdomlaneofwealth.com

Sorrowful, yet always rejoicing; poor, yet making many rich; having nothing, and yet possessing everything. **2 Corinthians 6:10**

Better a little with righteousness than much gain with injustice. **Proverbs 16:8**

The rich rule over the poor, and the borrower is slave to the lender. **Proverbs 22:7**

The wicked borrow and do not repay, but the righteous give generously. **Psalm 37:21**

After Job had prayed for his friends, the Lord restored his fortunes and gave him twice as much as he had before. **Job 42:10**

The seed falling among the thorns refers to someone who hears the word, but the worries of this life and the deceitfulness of wealth choke the word, making it unfruitful. **Matthew 13:22**

A person's riches may ransom their life, but the poor cannot respond to threatening rebukes. **Proverbs 13:8**

Believers in humble circumstances ought to take pride in their high position. But the rich should take pride in their humiliation—since they will pass away like a wild flower. **James 1:9-10**

Do not make any gods to be alongside me; do not make for yourselves gods of silver or gods of gold. **Exodus 20:23**

For bonuses go to ...

Bring the full tithe into the storehouse, that there may be food in my house. And thereby put me to the test, says the Lord of hosts, if I will not open the windows of heaven for you and pour down for you a blessing until there is no more need. **Malachai 3:10**

But if anyone does not provide for his relatives, and especially for members of his household, he has denied the faith and is worse than an unbeliever. **1 Timothy 5:8**

Give, and it will be given to you. Good measure, pressed down, shaken together, running over, will be put into your lap. For with the measure you use, it will be measured back to you." **Luke 6:38**

Precious treasure and oil are in a wise man's dwelling, but a foolish man devours it. **Proverbs 21:20**

A slack hand causes poverty, but the hand of the diligent makes rich. **Proverbs 10:4**

Come now, you rich, weep and howl for the miseries that are coming upon you. Your riches have rotted and your garments are moth-eaten. Your gold and silver have corroded, and their corrosion will be evidence against you and will eat your flesh like fire. You have laid up treasure in the last days. Behold, the wages of the laborers who mowed your fields, which you kept back by fraud, are crying out against you, and the cries of the harvesters have reached the ears of the Lord of hosts. You have lived on the earth in luxury and in self-indulgence. You have fattened your hearts in a day of slaughter. **James 5:1–6**

Behold, what I have seen to be good and fitting is to eat and drink and find enjoyment in all the toil with which one toils under the sun, the few days of his life that God has given him, for this is his lot. Everyone also to whom God has given wealth and possessions and power to enjoy them, and to accept his lot and rejoice in his toil—this is the gift of God. For he will not much remember the days of his life because God keeps him occupied with joy in his heart. **Ecclesiastes 5:18–20**

Know well the condition of your flocks and give attention to your herds. **Proverbs 27:23**

Whoever has a bountiful eye will be blessed, for he shares his bread with the poor. **Proverbs 22:9**

A stingy man hastens after wealth and does not know that poverty will come upon him. **Proverbs 28:22**

Beware of practicing your righteousness before other people in order to be seen by them, for then you will have no reward from your Father who is in heaven. Thus, when you give to the needy, sound no trumpet before you, as the hypocrites do in the synagogues and in the streets, that they may be praised by others. Truly, I say to you, they have received their reward. But when you give to the needy, do not let your left hand know what your right hand is doing, so that your giving may be in secret. And your Father who sees in secret will reward you. **Matthew 6:1–4**

For bonuses go to ...

Treasures gained by wickedness do not profit, but righteousness delivers from death. **Proverbs 10:2**

Jesus looked up and saw the rich putting their gifts into the offering box, and he saw a poor widow put in two small copper coins. And he said, "Truly, I tell you, this poor widow has put in more than all of them. For they all contributed out of their abundance, but she out of her poverty put in all she had to live on." **Luke 21: 1–4**

And all who believed were together and had all things in common. And they were selling their possessions and belongings and distributing the proceeds to all, as any had need. **Acts 2:44–45**

A false balance is an abomination to the Lord, but a just weight is his delight. **Proverbs 11:1**

Put no trust in extortion; set no vain hopes on robbery; if riches increase, set not your heart on them. **Psalm 62:10**

But Peter said to him, "May your silver perish with you, because you thought you could obtain the gift of God with money. **Acts 8:20**

Jesus said to him, "If you would be perfect, go, sell what you possess and give to the poor, and you will have treasure in heaven; and come, follow me." When the young man heard this, he went away sorrowful, for he had great possessions. And Jesus said to his disciples, "Truly, I say to you, only with difficulty will a rich person enter the kingdom of heaven. Again I tell you, it is easier for a camel to go through the eye of a needle than for a rich person to enter the kingdom of God." When the disciples heard this, they were greatly astonished, saying, "Who then can be saved?" **Matthew 19:21–26**

Remove far from me falsehood and lying; give me neither poverty nor riches; feed me with the food that is needful for me, lest I be full and deny you and say, "Who is the Lord?" or lest I be poor and steal and profane the name of my God. **Proverbs 30:8–9**

Therefore, I tell you, do not be anxious about your life, what you will eat or what you will drink, nor about your body, what you will put on. Is not life more than food, and the body more than clothing? **Matthew 6:25**

Such are the ways of everyone who is greedy for unjust gain; it takes away the life of its possessors. **Proverbs 1:19**

Now there is great gain in godliness with contentment, for we brought nothing into the world, and we cannot take anything out of the world. But if we have food and clothing; with these we will be content. But those who desire to be rich fall into temptation, into a snare, into many senseless and harmful desires that plunge people into ruin and destruction. For the love of money is the root of all kinds of evils. It is through this craving that some have wandered away from the faith and pierced themselves with many pangs. **1 Timothy 6:6–12**

Every man shall give as he is able, according to the blessing of the Lord your God that he has given you. **Deuteronomy 16:17**

For bonuses go to www.wisdomlaneofwealth.com

Whoever is greedy for unjust gain, troubles his own household, but he who hates bribes will live. **Proverbs 15:27**

For the protection of wisdom is like the protection of money, and the advantage of knowledge is that wisdom preserves the life of him who has it. **Ecclesiastes 7:12**

ABOUT THE AUTHOR

Francis Adu-Donkor has held positions as a Stewardship and Communications Leader at the Heritage Ghanaian Seventh Day Adventist Church in Toronto, Canada. His zeal for the kingdom work of God created a passion for him to delve deep into the spiritual aspects of wealth. His daily readings of the scriptures, about principles, keys and precepts of wealth creation and its subsequent divine use, changed his financial life completely.

Born into an average Ghanaian family of substandard economic and financial status, he knows what it means to be poor. But right from his infancy, he had a passion to flip this poverty status to a life filled with abundant wealth. This passion became more intense when he started life in Canada in March 2000. He left no stone unturned to be a manifestation of the Canadian dream, by being diligent in all spheres of life. Though he started life with barely anything financially, and initially lived in the slums of Toronto, he now counts himself blessed for implementing all the Biblical principles highlighted in his book. His obedience to the divine precepts made him unstoppable in terms of prosperity. It is his wish to share these principles with others who are still struggling to scratch out a daily existence.

www.ingramcontent.com/pod-product-compliance
Lightning Source LLC
Chambersburg PA
CBHW062204080426
42734CB00010B/1789